**This book is to be returned on or before
the last date stamped below.**

2 0 DEC 2002

D1422201

ASHGROVE PRESS, BATH

Published in Great Britain by
ASHGROVE PRESS LIMITED
7 Locksbrook Road Trading Estate
Bath BA1 3DZ

© Vanessa Davies and Hilary Andrew 1995

ISBN 1–85398–059–5

First published 1995

Typeset by
Ann Buchan (Typesetters), Middlesex
Printed by Redwood Books Ltd
Trowbridge, Wiltshire

To our beautiful daughters – we adore you
Harrie, Bridie and Hannah

To *Gordon*
Without whose loving care, my part in this book could
never have been written.
Sadly, he did not live to see it.

Carole

Vanessa Davies B.A Dip. App. Psy. R.S.A. (Coun)
Regular Member of the Institute of Transactional
Analysis is a psychologist and counsellor. She is
the author of *Abortion and Afterwards* (Ashgrove
Press) and is a lecturer and trainer on the topics
of counselling, sexual abuse and abortion. She
lives in Somerset with her twin daughters Hannah
and Bridie.

Hilary Andrew BSC. Applied Psychology Regular Member of the Institute of Transactional
Analysis is a psychologist and counsellor. She
has extensive experience as a Rape Crisis counsellor and working with adult survivors of
childhood sexual abuse. She has four children –
Sam, Toby, Harrie and Jonah – and lives in
Somerset.

ACKNOWLEDGEMENTS

Our first thank you must be to Carole. Carole is a very special, beautiful, brave person (believe us Carole!) who survived her appalling childhood. There are no words to describe her experience well enough. We salute you! and above all wish you joy, freedom and all the love you deserve.

Thank you to all the women who told us their experiences of childhood sexual abuse – for letting us know the adult you are and trusting us with the brave little girls you were.

To Nicky Burrows who is just brilliant at editing and commenting on our style, content etc. Your 'Be Perfect' driver is a friend to us all!

To Paul whose computing skills were of enormous value, especially when Gremlins attacked our systems (or was it us?) Anyway Paul was alway diplomatic and on hand night and day.

To Peter Redford for his time and expertise in editing the original manuscript.

To Julia Hewson – an inspiration and an excellent therapist who helped us remain friends through the writing of this book.

To Helen Phillips and Adie Russell for putting us in contact with some of the women in this book.

And to Gwen – Vanessa's nan – who taught her so much but sadly did not live to see this book in print.

CONTENTS

PREFACE

In 1991 we ran a group for women who had been sexually abused as children when, having been asked by Carole to find a therapist who could run a group, we realised as psychologists and counsellors we were able and motivated to do so. During the course of the group we and the women were struck by the lack of British resources – personal accounts, workbooks, books etc. There were good American publications but they reflected the language and culture of a different country; this made it difficult for the women to identify with what they were reading. We were all continuously making translations, and often the women were left feeling 'is this book really for me?'

The British books available were either textbooks written for therapists or presented as a recovery programme. What we felt were missing were answers to the questions most survivors ask, and what we believe is fundamental to overcoming and understanding the legacy of their abuse – 'why can't I put it behind me?' 'why me' 'how can what happiness to me now be about what happened then?' Having a shared psychotherapeutic training in Transactional Analysis meant we could use that as a basis for providing answers to these questions.

From the beginning it was our intention to include the experiences of women as we had felt the power of that sharing in the group. Carole has so eloquently given her story which is such an essential part of this book, and we love her dearly.

During the writing of this book there have been many changes both personal and political. Our understanding and awareness has grown whilst society struggles with just that. False Memory Syndrome has become the focus of abuse whilst behind the scenes hundreds of women help and are helped in their understanding and recovery. It is our hope that in some way this book adds to that.

Introduction

TERMS USED IN THE BOOK

There are many words and phrases we use throughout *Betrayal of Trust*. They were chosen for ease of reading, not to label people. Labels are restrictive and overlook the richness and complexity of people as individuals.

We decided, after discussion with women who were abused as children, to use the term 'survivor' to describe them as adults and 'victim' to describe them and others when we talk about their childhood experiences. We see the child as an innocent sufferer of abuse inflicted and perpetrated by others, while adults, who survived (many do not) have had an experience which could have easily killed them, caused them to kill themselves, go crazy or hurt others.

Obviously both sexes are abused, but this book concentrates on experiences of women survivors. However, men who have been abused will find aspects of the book useful and women's stories will reflect their own experiences.

To describe the abuser we have used 'he' and alternate the description of him between perpetrator and abuser, though we recognise that mothers, aunts, grandmothers, sisters and other women also abuse children.

We use the terms 'abusive' and 'good enough' families, but we acknowledge these are extremes. When abuse occurs in a family we label that family 'abusive' and when there is no abuse whatsoever we label the family 'good enough', but there are also families in which abuse is perpetrated by outsiders – baby-sitters, teachers, priests, family friends and so on. These families are neither 'abusive' nor 'good enough' and the reasons for this are outlined in the section 'The World of the Child'.

A few technical terms are used to refer to the theory behind the therapeutic approach we use, and these are explained when they appear in the text. Wherever possible, we have avoided using any psychological jargon, as this only hinders reading.

BETRAYAL OF TRUST

'As a child, as an innocent, you put your trust in adults and they betray you' Donna – a survivor.

In the 1990s we are witnessing the breakdown of one of the last taboos – childhood sexual abuse. Women's magazines carry articles, the major TV 'soaps' run stories of incest and abuse and school programmes tackle the issue as part of sex education. Socially, it is becoming a subject which no longer goes unmentioned. The few helplines available are being flooded with callers, mainly women, seeking help and a listening ear. The new, more accepting climate makes it easier for adults to acknowledge that children around them may be victims of abuse. There is an increased awareness of the behaviours and situations which may indicate that a child is suffering. Hopefully, children will be more able to speak out at the time and not have to carry the secret with them into adult life.

This illustrates how the new awareness is focused on children while adult survivors remain forgotten. To a certain degree statistics reveal how many women are abused; but they fail to show how individual women are affected. The pain and legacy of abuse do not diminish over time – each survivor always carries the hurt and loss within her. Society still expects her to have come to terms with it and to put it behind her.

For women who were victims of abuse in childhood this change in attitude may make it harder for them to disown their experience or minimise the effect it has had on their lives. Many women only break the silence in adulthood, while some never do. Some just want to forget, to put the past behind them, but society's increased awareness constantly brings up the past for them. To cope with the present they need to heal the past.

So, in these supposedly enlightened times, does society really know what sexual abuse is? We have become familiar with the term 'sexual abuse' but often only the victims and professionals have a genuine insight. Media reports never give details and often present a distorted view – one newspaper columnist recently described abuse as '. . . knee dangling uncles and kissing cousins. . . .' and a survivor as 'jumping on the bandwagon of abuse'.

When directly confronted by it we regard it with horror, disbelief and outrage. We tend to have a narrow-minded view: we think we know what it is but prevent ourselves from *really* knowing. We protect ourselves through denial because it is too shocking. Even academic definitions shield us from the reality of abuse: 'A child is sexually abused when another person, who is sexually mature, involves the child in any activity which the other person expects to lead to their sexual arousal. This might involve exposure of the sexual organs, touching, intercourse, showing pornographic material or talking about abuse in an erotic way.'*

Survivors may have experienced one or many incidents of abuse. These include kissing in a sexual way, kissing the child's body, touching, rubbing or licking the genitals, the abuser rubbing himself on the child, making the child watch him masturbate or making the child masturbate him, making the child masturbate herself, watching pornographic movies, taking pictures of the child in erotic poses, inserting fingers or other objects in her rectum or vagina, giving her or making her perform oral sex, ejaculating over her body or in her mouth, and vaginal or anal intercourse. The child may be abused by more than one person at the same time, or be abused while other children are present. Some victims will have endured tor-ture and abuse by groups of adults – cults.†

*Baker A W and Duncan S P (1985). Child Sexual Abuse: A Study of Prevalence in Great Britain. Child Abuse and Neglect, 9, 457–467.

† Satanic cults, whose participants worship Satan, are one example. There are other cults which abuse and torture children who are not connected to Satanism.

That is by no means a definitive list. It is included not to shock but because the abuser will often convince the child victim it is normal and acceptable. Victims may also minimise what is happening.

Sexual abuse is a misuse of power. It is an act of power and control which results in sexual gratification for the abuser. There can NEVER be an equal relationship between adults and child. No child can consent because she does not have the capacity to understand what she is consenting to.

Abuse is more often than not committed by family or friends of family – people in positions of trust. Children are taught to be careful about strangers in the street, but not about those they have a relationship with. The most common abuse is from father to daughter.

'This abuse happens any time an adult or near-adult takes away the child's right to exclusive ownership of her body. It is accomplished by manipulation of the child's feelings or by force. It ranges from making her feel daddy will be miserable unless he can fondle her, to brutal sexual assault. The child has lost power over her body, over her sexuality, over her very self.'*

A child can experience nothing so harmful emotionally and psychologically as sexual abuse from those she trusts – family members or people outside the family. The legacy the child takes into adulthood can include low self-esteem, feelings of failure or 'not being good enough', physical ailments, fears and phobias, dependency on food, drugs or alcohol, relationship and sexual problems, emotional instability and, for some, psychiatric illness and even suicide.

The fact that these children survived is a celebration in itself. *Betrayal of Trust* examines what happens to a child who has been sexually abused and how she grows into adulthood. It answers questions such as 'Why me?', 'Why did it happen in my family?' and 'Why didn't I tell?'. It looks at how a child copes and how her coping strategies

*Ellen Bass et al *I never told anyone* 1983 Harper and Row

create a pattern she carries into adult life. It looks at how women who are abused as children relate to others and themselves in terms of relationships, family, sexuality and so on. It shows how it is possible to confront the abuse by acknowledging its impact on the present and making sure it can no longer affect the future. It shows how it is possible to move from being a victim to a survivor, regaining trust and control over life and relationships with others.

It is not our intention to label women survivors as damaged, unstable or suicidal people, although children who are subjected to experiences which are terrifying and humiliating can not escape emotional injury.

As we shall see, abuse takes place in families which do not allow certain feelings, do not communicate well, have few rules, and few or no boundaries, have confusion over the roles of their members, have little affection or have little space for individuality. Love is only given conditionally, if at all. Those who should have cared for their child have violated her. Those who should have protected her have ignored her. Those who should have loved her have betrayed her. The abuser dishonours her trust by threatening, lying, and manipulating her into doing things which frighten and hurt her.

Children are compliant and trusting, it is easy for an adult to abuse their trust. When trust is broken by someone the child loves, believes in and relies on it can destroy her ability to trust again. The devious tactics of the abuser may leave the child with little understanding of trust. Consequently adults can no longer be depended on, and their actions and words become meaningless or inconsistent. The child's lack of trust is carried into all her relationships later in life.

Every relationship we have depends on trust and the level of intimacy we develop with that person. Intimacy comes from trust, so you can not be intimate with someone you do not believe in. If we learn from our parents that it is OK to love and be close we will grow up able to do this as adults.

Children who are abused suffer a double tragedy. They are denied true loving touch by being abused – but because of the abuse there is a greater need for real emotional intimacy.

The survivor may not know what trust is because her experience of trusting relationships is often non-existent. She has learned that people are not what they seem. For trust to develop, life has to be consistent. Some survivors may feel they do trust people but their's is often a naïve and indiscriminate trust: they have not learned to distinguish between who can be trusted and who can not.

As an adult the survivor's inability to trust anyone prevents her from seeking help, which in turn leads to feelings of isolation. The more isolated she becomes, the more difficult it is to begin making relationships and for trust to develop.

For the survivor, the world becomes an unsafe place where no-one can be trusted. Consequently, the need to control others and the world becomes all-important – 'if I am in control nothing can hurt me'. This control may be achieved through working too much, needing to get everything right, not allowing other to do things for her, being excessively tidy and organised and so on.

For the child who is not abused trusting the world, others and herself – her thoughts, feelings and perceptions – is easier. A child is naturally trusting – it is one of the most basic instincts. She knows when someone is lying or being false. She has a basic awareness of what is right and wrong. For the child victim this can lead to confusion because her intuitive knowledge and her experience conflict. In later life this can lead to feelings of craziness and in order to control the conflict she may separate from her feelings completely. It is possible as an adult to relay those foundations which should have been laid in childhood. She can learn to trust herself again.

A child who is abused does not stand out – she is normal, no more or less pretty, precocious, stupid or vulnerable than any other child. It is the abuser who makes her a victim. He violates her mind and body and takes away her innocence and her right to be a child. It is unlikely that he will recognise what he has done and, even more so, that he will assume responsibility for his horrendous acts. Nothing can undo the betrayal of trust.

VICTIM TO SURVIVOR

'As a child you are a victim – it is the only word which stresses the point that this was something done to you when you didn't do something wrong in the beginning. At the end of the day you do survive. There is living proof that you do go on with your life. You have to survive it. I'm proud to use the term' *Donna*

The adult survivor of childhood sexual abuse has been cheated of her childhood, her body and her peace of mind. She feels compelled to keep her secret and is shamed into silence. She punishes herself for the sin she feels she has committed, never allowing people to see her real self because they wouldn't want to know her. She has become the person who other people want her to be and ignores her own needs and desires, if she knows them. She discounts her own feelings, intuition and perceptions as unimportant. She may endure paralysing depressions and swings of emotion, fearing she is going crazy. Sometimes she turns to suicide as a way out, or drugs, alcohol, self inflicted wounds, sex or food to numb the pain. Her daytime is filled with feelings of not being good enough, guilt, being responsible, damaged, soiled, full of self-loathing, unable to feel she is coping.

She has been robbed of the power to protect and look after herself. She has been robbed of the knowledge that she deserves safety. She is touched by inexplicable fear. She may have intense reactions to a certain place, certain people. She may be plagued by nightmares, attacks of panic and recurrent illness. She seeks love and affection but does not allow herself to become close. She can not say no or ask for what she wants, always blames herself when things go wrong. She feels she has nothing to offer others and returns to people who hurt her again and again. She copes alone, not expecting others to care or help. She is isolated in a life where she feels no-one sees her. She feels incomplete and unhappy.

'To continue to call her a 'victim' is to insult her by overlooking the victory of her survival'*

The women who have shared their stories in this book, despite the violation of their minds and bodies, are SUR-VIVORS. Their experiences as children were harrowing, cruel, bewildering, and often life-threatening. They were profoundly hurt and affected, not by strangers, but people they loved and trusted. They were not unusual or extra-ordinary children. They were normal but born into abusive families or ones which were unable to protect them. Like thousands of other victims of childhood sexual abuse they were taught, often through physical and emotional abuse, to keep their ordeal and pain a secret. For some this meant many years of silence. They were the victims who survived, who didn't let the abuse cause them to kill themselves, hurt others or go crazy, even though they may have felt like doing so many times.

They, like you, had a will to live and carry on despite everything.

Many survivors fail to recognise the healing they have already achieved by living through their childhood.

You, like them, have already survived the worst part. You are not alone. You are not crazy. It was not your fault. It IS possible to heal. There is no cure but there is recov-ery.*

As you heal you will discover that the world is NOT a totally unsafe place. Life can be enjoyable you can ex-plore, be loved, be free from your fears, you can feel your feelings, share your experiences and thoughts with others and know they feel the same, know that people care about you, that you are loveable, that you are important.

*Beverley Engel – *The Right to Innocence* Ivy Books.

INSIDE STORIES

We talked in-depth to three survivors – Carole, Donna and Sue – and questionnaires were used with five other women. We could not include everything they told us, but parts have been chosen which illustrate the points we wish to make. The quotes in the book are direct – only minor changes have been made to make them more readable.

We respected each woman's right to decide whether she wanted her name used or not. Some had reasons, including fear of personal or legal retribution, which prevented them from doing so but did not prevent them from being part of this book. Carole is able to use her full name because her abuser was prosecuted.

All the women have been engaged in some form of therapy and feel they have started their healing process.

The book concentrates on recovery because it IS possible. A book only about effects would have left readers stranded with other people's histories as well as their own, without showing them healing is possible.

Carole

Carole is in her early fifties. She has a married daughter and a son. She was one of five children. She had a large extended family and her grandmother lived with her parents. Carole was sexually abused from the ages of 6 to 16 years by her father. He was regularly physically violent to Carole and her mother and verbally abusive to his own mother. She disclosed at the age of 16 to a Sunday School teacher which resulted in her father's conviction and imprisonment for 2 years – he only served 13 months. She has had individual therapy and, recently, group therapy and has reached the final stages of her healing process.

She eloquently sums up her experience of abuse and her recovery from the effects:

I knew something was stopping me from being a

'normal' human being. I was crying too easily, having nightmares, broken relationships and strong feelings that I was a horrible person. For forty years the abuse affected my entire life, but doesn't have to any more. I will never forget – how could I ever forget – such savage violation of my mind and body? However, I have learned that I am loveable, and that I have control over my body, my mind and my life. I have the right to exist, to say yes AND no, to be happy, and to ask for and expect what I need and want in personal relationships. I do not have to accept anything less. BEING USED AND ABUSED WAS NOT AND NEVER WILL BE NORMAL OR ACCEPTABLE.

Carole's story, which runs through this book and illustrates the process of healing, is one of a violated terrifying childhood which haunted her until recently. Her courageous and sensitive account is proof that healing is possible, whatever your age. She found a way to shed the feelings from the past which were still affecting her present and preventing her from being happy, whole and in control.

We chose her story because, as her therapists, we were able to comment on her therapy. Her story covers most aspects of abuse and recovery.

Donna

Donna is in her late thirties. She lives with her cat and has one son and a grandson. She was part of a large family, with 5 stepbrothers, a twin brother and a younger sister. Her father left the family when she was ten, and she describes him as an alcoholic womaniser who beat his wife. Donna was abused from four years old by two of her brothers, later by a neighbour and in her early teens by a married couple.

When she was 12 a local man tried to rape her at knife point. Memories of abuse only surfaced in her early thirties when her mother died, though she always knew she had been abused. She thinks her sister was abused also.

She joined a group of other survivors with whom she was able to talk about her childhood.

Sue

Sue is in her in forties, and lives with her partner and one of her two daughters. She was one of a family of four children and was abused by her father from the ages of 9 to 13 years. Sue also remembered the abuse but does not know if it happened to any of her siblings. The abuse just stopped – she did not know why. She nursed her mother for nearly two years before she died. Her father became more dependent on her and because of this she had to confront him. It also meant she had to tell her family. Like Donna she found comfort and support in group therapy with other survivors.

The book is for you, from them. They are, as you are, the experts.

AIMS

This books aims to –

- break the taboo of silence by further bringing the subject of abuse out into the open
- to help women understand that they did not deserve to be abused, were not to blame, and can recover
- to acknowledge the suffering of women – and to demystify the healing process.
- The basic theme is how the abuse hurt and affected you and how you can understand, explain and heal from the effects in your adult life.

The book charts the experience of survivor from childhood to adulthood. The survivor may use it to help her grieve the for losses of her childhood and move on with other women through the affirmation that healing is possible. They were not to blame. They are OK.

The book looks at how sexual abuse has affected women and the impact of abuse on their lives and personalities – so you can begin to see how you became the person you are today with your individual problems and ways of coping. We want you to realise your own strengths and move on from outdated ways of coping. We provide a framework for understanding so that you may step out of patterns which run your lives.

When asking women survivors what they would like from the book they unanimously agreed that they would like to have access to other women's stories, 'real' accounts of women's experiences: how they had coped and how they had overcame the effects. Tracy wanted a book which 'gives personal accounts, no scientific, long words, something basic but deep enough to allow you to cry, to make you think and give you support. A victim needs love, support and a time to cry'.

We wanted to provide a book which helps. All the women in the book wanted to tell their stories to help other women who still suffer in silence, and do not know or believe healing is possible. Their stories are of long-term invasion and extensive sexual abuse. You may have had a similar experience, or one episode of abuse but PLEASE don't discount your experience and think this book isn't for you. ANY ABUSE IS BAD and can have the same long-lasting effects. For the women involved, although being part of the book is part of their healing process, their main motivation is to help other women.

The book has a lot of pain in it – a book about child sexual abuse can not gloss over the facts. We wanted to explore the heart of the experience without sensationalising it or being voyeuristic. As Donna says 'The truth not a story book'.

YOU AND THE BOOK

The stories are not definitive accounts, but are included

for you to find recognition and comfort. There will be differences between your story and those of the women in the book, but don't discount your's. The book is for YOU, too.

If you were abused you have come a long way merely by opening the book. Picking it up is an important step to confronting your past, beginning to break the secrecy and isolation, and connecting your past experience with the present.

You may have only a vague feeling something happened to you and feel scared or anxious when you are touched in a certain way, when you are in a certain situation or when you experience a certain smell. You may remember in full exactly what happened. Either way you will still be suffering from the legacy of abuse as an adult, something which will not simply go away. Feelings of shame, guilt, pain and fear are never far away.

You may have no memories, some women don't or if you do remember you may feel ashamed to tell anyone about it. You may feel it is all behind you now. What you do is for a very good reason, you are protecting yourself. When you are ready you will be able to look at your past.

You may, for your own reasons, fear facing the echoes of your past and hearing other women's stories. You may fear re-experiencing the feelings you have kept a lid on for so long, or not sensing any resolution and progress. You may fear being overwhelmed by your memories and emotions or, conversely, wanting to remember but not being able to do so.

You may fear that 'if I delve into this what would other people think' 'Will this mean I have to tell people I haven't told before' 'How will things change if I deal with this now?'

Reaching for help is never easy, especially for survivors. You may have developed many skills to help you survive and cope with your experience. Many women disown their feelings, their experience, the effect of that experience or minimise the impact it has had on them by saying 'it wasn't that bad' 'he only touched me, he didn't penetrate me'. Giving up these ways of surviving is scary and means you will have to go through the pain of your pent up feelings.

Feelings are our greatest allies in healing. Do not be afraid of them. They will guide you in your healing and let you know what you need to do. Feelings can not hurt you, by expressing them you can begin to have control over them. Feeling is a NATURAL process.

Recovery is not easy. There is no easy and quick solution to the pain you are feeling, but you are not alone. Many women have been where you are now and have been able to move forward.

Reading this book will have many effects on you and have a knock on effect on others – those with whom you live and mix. It may bring up feelings which you have suppressed or you may experience new feelings that you were unaware of. This may lead to you needing to withdraw from people close to you or desperately wanting more comfort and help. You may find yourself crying easily and having rapid changes of mood. You may feel as you did as a child, confused and unsure of how to cope. You may have difficulty in thinking clearly and experience intrusions of past memories. You may remember whole chunks of a past you had 'forgotten' and become uncomfortable in certain situations.

You may re-evaluate your relationships or behave differently with those close to you and those around you. This may be problematic at first but in the long run will be beneficial for you. As Carol* says 'it affected every part of my life, my job went, my relationships evaluated, friendships looked at, every part was re-evaluated'.

You may want to tell people of your experience or confront your abuser and your family.

You may increase your need to turn to drink, drugs, sex, food, hurting yourself, filling up your time to stop yourself from thinking and feeling what you are experiencing.

You have the choice of being able to discover how you

---

* Carol is not Carole but both wish to use their own names.

can begin to trust again, reclaim yourself, be intimate, be joyful and spontaneous. If you decide to heal then you will need to release your feelings and confront your shadows. You can not change the past but you can heal from it.

Although some women may find this book therapeutic it is not a substitute for individual or group counselling or group therapy. This does not mean women can not heal themselves with the support of friends and family, but often full recovery often requires help from someone who is not personally involved with you. Everyone will be at a different place when they read this, and everyone's healing will take a different length of time. If you are not ready yet to seek help from others you can start your healing here and follow our guidelines for keeping yourself safe.

Women may approach their healing in many different ways over the years. Carole had read books, undergone individual therapy and joined a group with other survivors, and she is now part of a self-help group. Other women find it useful to keep journals of their thoughts, feelings and dreams during healing. For some, writing an account of what happened to them is important and helps trigger further memories and recollections. It is up to you how you choose to go through your healing.

SAFETY

Feeling safe is a basic human right. It is essential to create safety for yourself. This involves understanding how reading this book will affect you and how others have created safety for themselves.

Even having created safety for yourself, reading this book may be difficult and at times painful. But it will never be as traumatic as your childhood experience. This time YOU are in control. You can choose when and for how long and under what circumstances you want to relive your past through these chapters.

You are the best judge of your healing process.

There are many ways of protecting yourself while reading this book and remaining in control, even though you may experience some of the effects we have listed. Some of the women whose stories are in this book have used these while understanding and overcoming their past. You may like to try some of the following ideas in order to keep you safe and in control.

Decide when and where you want to read this book – choose a time and place which feel safe for you, or at least feel comfortable. You may never have experienced privacy as a child and decide to read this book when you are alone, or you may feel you need support and ask a friend to be with you while you read. You might like to choose somewhere that is safe for you: a favourite chair, a particular place in your home or outside your house, you may want to have something with you that has special meaning. Decide what you want and need .

When you have finished reading the book, create a ritual to symbolise that you have had enough of it for now: for example, make a cup of tea, have a bath, listen to some music, go for walk, and so on.

This book can not be a substitute for personal or group therapy and if you experience dramatic shifts of feeling, thinking and behaviour approach a therapist, counsellor or someone, close to help you.

The World of the Child

Carole

'My father was born in Canada, as his father was in the Canadian navy at the time. He was one of seven children, his mother's favourite and thoroughly spoilt. As an adult he often abused his mother verbally and she made no attempt to stand up to him.

She died at the age of 45. My paternal grandparents lived apart for some years. I do not remember them being together. My grandfather drank a great deal and according to information from the family, abused his elder daughter in her teens. This apparently ended when she left home. I believe my father knew of this.

My mother, was cared for by her step-sister Mary for some years. Mary's husband was in the Navy, often away for long periods. She appeared to me to be strong and capable, and she provided us with a home for a while. I remember living in several different places, our first real family home being a prefab in Bath, where the abuse began.

My parents were just 17 when I was born. When I was 13 my mother told me they had had to get married because she was expecting me. This made me feel guilty, believing the problems they appeared to have were my fault. I have often thought my mother might not have married my father if she had not become pregnant. My mother wanted a boy with each of her pregnancies. Ironically, the only boy she had died of a heart attack at the age of 35. She was devastated and when I took her to place flowers on his grave one Sunday afternoon she talked to him as if they were alone together. I had to walk away because it was so sad.

I was the first grandchild in my father's family. My aunts and uncles were all very good to me. I saw very little of my father until I was 4 or 5 because of the war –

he was abroad with the RAF. My father is selfish, intolerant, brutal, domineering, cruel, inpatient, cowardly, moody, inconsiderate, lazy, emotional at times, and devious. I have seen him cry for a fox hunted down by hounds but I have also seen him beat our lovely dog with a stick – he pretended the dog broke its leg falling down the side of a quarry but I always knew that wasn't so.

He was a talented artist, drawing mainly wildlife, portraits of film stars and self-portraits. He was gifted in other ways – he was an excellent photographer who built his own camera, enlarger and even a telescope, and he could also make beautiful things in wood. He was so clever but I can never remember him having a skilled job.

If we had experienced a normal father/daughter relationship I know it would have been good. It could have been so different. It does not make me angry, just sad that he deprived us both of that.

My father was, and still is to some extent, a bastard to my mother showing her no affection or respect. My mother is quiet, subservient and weak, though I have often thought her weakness was her strength because it enabled her to endure his treatment for so many years. She should have left him years ago. She has always done everything to keep the peace and lives life on a purely superficial level, where nothing of any importance is ever mentioned, let alone discussed. She has always been afraid to show her feelings about anything to anyone, but despite this she now has close and loving relationships with some of her grandchildren – I think they are a great comfort to her.

I do not remember my father and brother getting on well. My brother was very close to my mother and had no respect for my father because of the way he treated her, yet sometimes he would sit up all night playing chess with him. My brother, John, died at 35 because he abused his body. He was overweight, and smoked and drank heavily. I thought he did this as a result of a broken relationship, and maybe that was a contributing factor, but now I have other views. He collapsed in the street on the way to the pub for a Sunday lunch-time drink. The ambulance driver stopped at my mother's house to ask if she wanted to go to the hospital with him but she could not do it. I think she has regretted that decision ever since.

My paternal grandmother lived with us for most of the time. My father was more often than not unemployed and my grandmother helped finance the family. He appreciated nothing, yet when she died he sat in my house and cried, but I could not rescue him. I felt angry with him for the way he had treated her and had taken her for granted for so long.

My mother was totally dominated by my father and he often physically abused her. I remember him turning her out of the house in the middle of winter when she was 7 months pregnant. I've seen him turn a full table of food and crockery upside down in a rage and take a hatchet to the furniture. I think my grandmother was quite dominant too. She and my mother managed to live together without having a cross word. My mother was so passive she never complained about anything — it seems her role in life has always been to please others.

Before he started abusing me when I was 6, I thought my father was wonderful. I remember him taking me to see my brother when he was born, sitting me on his knee and asking me if I liked my baby brother. He was smiling down at me and I loved him then. I believed my parents were happy then.

I do not remember being cuddled or kissed by my parents as a child. When I was 7 or 8 my mother kissed me once when I gave her some flowers on Mothers Day. She cried too.

I often had to look after my sister Lana, who is 8 years younger than me, and I really resented that. When I was about nine my mother told me I shouldn't grumble when I was asked to help in the house because she had grumbled with her mother, and when her mother died she was very sorry. It made me feel guilty – it was a kind of punishment.

When I was punished it took the form of smacking, being deprived of my freedom, not being allowed to go out to play or attend the church group, which was my refuge, or listen to my favourite radio programmes. I was always surprised when aunts and uncles were nice to me. I always felt different and I really wanted to be like everyone else. I never felt part of that family – I felt like a stranger.

CHILDHOOD

In order to understand the impact of abuse on the adult we need first to return to the world of the child.

> A baby requires the certainty that *she* will be protected in every situation, that *her* arrival is desired, that *her* cries are heard, that the movements of *her* eyes are responded to and *her* fears calmed. The baby needs assurance that *her* hunger and thirst will be satisfied, *her* body lovingly cared for, and *her* distress never ignored.*

From the day you were born you were a princess – you were beautiful and OK. Your stance was one of basic trust, you were worthy, and important simply because you existed. You were entitled to be loved just for being YOU.

You were born to grow, to love, to trust, to have fun, to express your feelings and to get your demands met. You were capable of 'unqualified love, of spontaneous joy and of straight thinking'.† You needed to know you were loved – unconditionally, to know you mattered, that you would be taken care of, that you had a right to be alive, that you were important. You needed love and attention just as much as you needed food. Without food you would have died physically and without love and affection you would have died psychologically.‡

* Alice Miller – *Banished Knowledge,* Virago Press (1991). Italics indicate where we have changed gender from 'his' to 'her'.

† *Transactional Analysis In Management* Julie Hewson and Colin Turner, The Staff College Page 83 (1992).

‡ 'There is a minimal level of necessary stroking (Nurturing) below which the child may not survive. It pines away with a malady known to Victorians as marasmus or withering' from Julie Hewson and Colin Turner *Transactional Analysis In Management* (1992) The Staff College. Our brackets

You relied on your parents to teach you about the world and yourself – you were born trusting because you had no choice. You were supposed to be demanding and, as is normal, as far as you were concerned the world revolved around you.

You had the potential, like all babies, to bloom into a healthy person but you could not learn by yourself. You were at the mercy of others. As a child you were 'a two-foot creature who is totally dependent upon big six-foot godlike creatures who literally have the power of life and death' over you.* Your childhood and future adult life depended on which type of family you were born into. You can choose your friends but not your family.

Those babies born into families, which were 'abusive' or NOT 'good enough', may have been victims of incest or sexual abuse, physical or emotional abuse from the time they were born.

If like Carole, Donna and Sue you were born into an abusive family you may, even from the very beginning, have had to cope with and make sense of experiences which threatened your mind and body.

Our childhood experiences create our sense of reality about ourselves and the world. As one writer says: 'A human being born into a cold, indifferent world will regard *her* situation as the only one possible. Everything that person later comes to believe, advocate, and deem right is founded on *her* first formative experiences'.†

The baby's main task is to identify her needs and how to get them met. She has to compromise her own needs to get along with her parents – she learns how best to get by in the world. A child born into an 'abusive' family quickly learns that the world is not moulded around her – she must fit in with others.

As one writer describes it 'Being born into a family is like coming late to a party where everyone has been

---

* 'A Developmental Therapeutic Roadmap', Vann Joines Transactional Analysis Journal 6:2 April 1976.

† Alice Miller – *Banished Knowledge*, Virago Press, 1991. (Our italics)

talking, dancing, joking, eating, smoking and drinking for hours. If the first year of life is welcoming, the child believes, 'I should be at this party. It is all right that I exist. I do not have to prove my worth or justify my existence.' If the first year of life is not welcoming then the infant believes, 'Something has gone very wrong. My being causes other people unhappiness. I should not exist. I must prove my worth. I must justify my existence.*

Before Carole was abused her perception of her family was one of happy times. She talks about her father putting her on his knee and welcoming her baby brother. But from Carole's description of the family we can see there were many indicators to show she was born into an 'abusive' family, even though her early memories tell her things were happy enough.

This is normal and in most cases the child doesn't know her family is 'abusive'. The compulsion for her is to believe they are OK. As Donna says 'I suppose at the time I thought it was a normal family as there was nothing abnormal about it, as far as I could see, because I lived in it. When I look back my dad used to beat my mum up and was an alcoholic – at the time it was normal. Looking back though things were not normal – nobody ever talked to each other.'

We know that Carole's paternal grandfather was an alcoholic and abused his own daughter, of which her own father was aware. Her paternal grandmother was a dominant woman who left her husband. Carole's mother had experienced the loss of her mother at a crucial age and was bought up by her step-sister.

Her parents were very young to take on the emotional and financial responsibility of marriage and family and relied on her grandmother for money and a roof over their heads. We also know her father did not have the motivation to take care of his family and left it up to his mother.

Carole's mother was weak and passive while her father was dominant and aggressive and was physically abusive.

* Linda Sanford – *Strong at the Broken Places* Virago Press, 1991, p. 119.

Within such a family it would have been important for Carole to have been as quiet and as undemanding as possible and to fit in with the other women and children in the household and provide for her father's needs.

Within the 'abusive' family the child has to adapt totally to her parents' demands, expectations and wishes. She becomes accomplished at reading parental clues and goes along with the rules. As Tracy says, 'My father's attitude and dominant personality stopped each member of the family communicating, he ruled everyone and blinded us from the truth with lies, threats and deceptions'.

She learns quickly that she is not loved for who she is but rather for what she can do. She becomes who her parents want her to be – an adult, a mother, a lover for her father, a scapegoat, a problem solver, cook, cleaner and so on. She has to grow up fast because being a child is dangerous.

Like other children born into abusive families, Carole quickly learned that her parents needs were placed above her own (and other people's). Unlike the child from the 'good enough' family she was not allowed to have a separate identity from her parents. They didn't allow her to have her own feelings and thoughts. Her father saw her as an extension of himself and controlled her – even the rights over her own body belonged to others.

Carole

'The acts of abuse included masturbating him, having to dress in my mother's underwear, rape, regular full intercourse, beatings, sleep deprivation, being left naked in a field, being locked in the bathroom with my father in the dark, having delayed exposure photographs taken with him having intercourse with me in a wood, and much more.

My first experience of abuse was in the bedroom of the prefab we were about to move into. My father told me to rub his penis, which was already hard. I had to do it until his breathing changed and the white stuff spurted out. My arm ached and I closed my eyes. I couldn't believe he had showed himself to me, never mind made me touch him.

To make sense of it that first time I thought it would bring peace for everyone. I thought it was horrible and I didn't like it, but felt I had to do it or life would be hell.

I felt numb, scared and unable to fully take in what had happened. I felt let down, hurt, confused and abandoned. I couldn't know it would be the start of ten years of agony. I wonder sometimes what I would have done if I had known what lay ahead for me.

I trained myself not to think about the abuse between the 'attacks'. He always said 'it won't hurt and it won't take long'. When I was really little – six or seven, he used to promise me treats and unrealistic rewards if I co-operated. They meant nothing because I knew I'd have to do it anyway. If I didn't cooperate life would be hell, not just for me but for my mother, too – he'd pick a fight with her over nothing because he hadn't been able to have his own way with me. I soon learned that it was easier and brought a little respite if I closed my mind and co-operated.

My mind and body had to be separate. I couldn't allow myself to think and feel at the same time. While

being abused I would shut my mind down completely –
I don't know how I did it, but if I hadn't I could not have
coped. I was always sure it would end one day – I didn't
know how, but I dared not give up hope. I think I would
have died of despair or gone crazy if I had .

I was threatened with violence and possible death if
I told anyone – I was even afraid of telling my mother. I
didn't realise for many years that she must have known,
which was a definite block. I can't be angry with her
though, because I feel so sorry for her, sorry that she's
so weak in some ways.

My father used various tactics to carry out his abuse,
encouraging my mother to go out so we were left alone,
cornering me in the bathroom and not going to work
during the school holidays so I had no escape. He
would also send me notes telling me to meet him in the
field at night with threats if I didn't do it.

He tried to make me ask him for sex, and kept me up
all night once or twice because I wouldn't – he wanted
to pretend he was my boyfriend. He wouldn't let me
have boyfriends – I was left naked in a field as punishment for being too friendly with a boy called Brian. After
I had been in the field for some time he returned, told
me to get dressed and drove me home, telling me I was
never to speak to Brian again. We walked into the
house as if nothing had happened – he had that much
power.

I thought if I did not make a fuss my father might stop
abusing me, but I soon learned it made no difference.
He had to be in control. He liked to control me – he even
made me drink sherry at my aunt's house when I was
15, knowing I did not like it.

I used to stay at school for as long as possible and
dreaded the holidays. I didn't do too well at school but
I liked it – it was safe and it WASN'T home. I got on quite
well with people in authority – a little in awe of them but
not scared and I became very attached to a male
teacher at junior school.

I soon realised I was different from other children. I

wanted their freedom more than anything. They never seemed under any kind of pressure and were always at ease with their parents and with life. My parents were strangers to me.

My feelings were totally ignored as a child, and I withdrew. I hardly ever cried. I wasn't praised for my achievements but was made to feel useless when I failed my 11 plus exam. So much was expected of me but in return I was given just ignorance and abuse.

I was never allowed to make my own decisions, always having to ask permission and too being frightened to be angry or to cry. There was a kind of safety in being treated badly, because at least I knew what to expect.

The only nurturing I ever received was being clothed and fed. I was never a child, in that I never felt young. I seemed to have lived a lifetime by the time I started Senior school.

My main attachments outside the family were the chapel and Gordon, my Sunday school teacher. He often said: 'Carole, you always look so sad. Is there anything you want to tell me?' I didn't identify it as sadness then, but looking back I can see he was right. He didn't need to be told I was being abused, but he couldn't help me because I wouldn't admit it.

I longed to be like other children, who had fathers who played normal games with them and didn't take them to places they didn't like. I was always frightened of my father. I was constantly threatened not to tell anyone. We were in the countryside one evening and he told me never to allow myself to be examined internally by anyone. There were always secrets to be kept.

I always had to pretend nothing was wrong. I wanted to be anywhere but in that family. When my sister was taken seriously ill with severe diabetes at the age of 8, I actually wished it had been me so I could escape. That may seem a wicked thing to want but I could only see it as freedom.

However, I always believed the abuse would end. It

was a strange kind of optimism. It is called survival. I thought it would end when I went into hospital to have my tonsils removed. I thought my father would leave me alone if I was not well. I even stopped wetting the bed in hospital – I was 8. Wetting the bed always meant trouble, as if it were deliberate. The doctor said I was lazy and no-one thought to investigate further.

In the early days of the abuse my father would often become upset and say he had not meant to do it. He cried sometimes and promised he would not do it again. Perhaps that is where my optimism came from that one day he might actually keep to his word. I didn't want to believe he wouldn't, but, as time went by he became more sure of himself and more familiar with his abuse, and the things he did became more serious.

Mine was a false life. I didn't like knowing the things I knew at such an early age. I knew about babies and intercourse when I was 7 or 8 years old. My father asked me one day if I knew what intercourse meant. I said I didn't and when he explained it to me he said that was what he was going to do to me when I was old enough – and he did, regularly. I didn't want to know these things and at Junior school I remember my friends discussing how babies were made and born. Some of them were so way off the mark. I wanted to say 'You know nothing about it – this is what happens', but I didn't want to admit I knew. I didn't want to have that knowledge because it made me feel different.

The abuse was never used as punishment – it happened anyway, whether I was good or bad. The punishment I received for not co-operating with him though was different. I was beaten, deprived of sleep, given no peace and never left alone.

One of our prefab windows looked out onto the front lawn. I remember my father wanting me to take my friend Daphne to play there. He wanted me to ask her to look in the window where he had stripped naked. I wouldn't do it and I was punished. It frightened me that he might do to her what he had done to me.

I was made to sleep with my father when my mother went into hospital to give birth to one of my sisters. I was forced to have intercourse with him every night. This is when I threw myself down the stairs hoping to injure myself enough to have to go to hospital – it didn't work. Another time I tried to injure myself was when he was driving me into the countryside late one night in a temper. I knew I was going to have a hard time and I tried to jump out of the van as it was moving, but he saw me and dragged me back. He then stopped in the gateway of a field and made me climb over the gate. When I refused he dragged me through the gate and I fell. Though I wanted to hurt myself enough to be taken away from him I didn't ever actually think I wanted to die. I just knew it would end someday.

Sometimes I tried to persuade my brother or sister to sleep in my bed, and I would cuddle them in such a way my father would have to wake them up in order to get me out of bed. I thought it would deter him but it didn't.

My father used the bathroom as a darkroom for his photography, so it was often blacked out. It was one of the places he would take me. I have a fear of water, or I thought it was the water I was frightened of, but I think it was the bathroom and its association with being abused. I often had to have someone to sit with me while I got into the bath, because of the fear. I had feelings of panic and the water seemed to take my breath away. I thought I was frightened of drowning but I was just vulnerable and being naked made those feelings stronger.

My early experiences and beliefs were that I was unlovable, unimportant, worthless and invisible – just there to be used and abused. I felt completely controlled and in my father's power, but at the same time abandoned, unprotected and sacrificed for the sake of peace in the everyday lives of the rest of the family.

I have always been able to sleep in times of trouble simply because I was deprived of it so much as a child. It is a kind of refuge, blocking out the problems for a few hours – a release. Being woken at night was worse than being cornered during the day. It seemed as if nowhere was safe and there was, no escape at all.

I have never neglected my appearance, mainly because I would feel I was letting myself down. I have yearned for approval of my clothes, hair, work, anything, but I was never taught to care for myself. I was never given even the most basic necessities, such as sanitary towels, deodorant, or a bra when I needed one. I remember stealing a bra from my mothers draw and wearing it till it was so dirty I couldn't wear it any longer. My mother couldn't seem to cope with my needs as I grew up, and I felt ashamed and shy of expressing them. When I had my periods I was given pieces of old towel for protection. I probably wore the same piece of towel for about three days, which smelt disgusting and made me so sore all the skin round my vagina peeled away. My first deodorant was given to me by my aunty Jane, who used to visit me when I lived in Southsea. She and my uncle Frank were very good to me – they cared when no-one else did. When I gave birth to my son I was seriously ill, not expected to live through the night and, though my parents were told, my mother wasn't allowed to visit me. Instead my aunt and uncle came to hospital to see me. They have helped me in many ways over the years – always there with their support and never judgmental – and I will always remember that.

I was chubby as a little girl, and a size 14 till I married and had my son. I then lost weight and have been a size 12 ever since. I have often tried to lose a few pounds but have never had any eating problems.

I was generally very healthy as a child, except for recurring tonsillitis till I was 8, though I remember feeling seriously ill at school when I was about 12 or 13, aching all over, feeling faint and very hot, but I wanted to stay at school because my father was at home and I didn't want to be there. Eventually the doctor had to call – I had a very bad bout of flu.

I am sure my brothers and sisters were not abused by my father. I sometimes wonder if my sister Lana would have been a victim had she not been ill and in hospital a great deal from the age of 8. There are eight years between Lana and my two younger sisters. One was born just before I left, the other afterwards. By that time my father had been to prison – if he hadn't been convicted my sisters might also have been abused, but I can never be sure of that.

When the intercourse started at the age of 12 he took precautions, using condoms which he made me watch him wash out for the next time. When my period was late he didn't appear to be worried, certainly not for me. Had I become pregnant an abortion would probably been arranged, but when my periods started he just said 'That little problem is over then'. He was relieved for himself – my feelings as usual, didn't matter.

BETRAYAL

'The moment a parent sexually abuses a child, that child becomes an orphan. the child loses the security of the abusing parent and loses the protection and trust of the parent who didn't stop it from happening'*

Sexual abuse causes immense distress, terror, discomfort and confusion to the child.

People the child loved and trusted invaded their personal boundaries, used their tiny, or immature, bodies for their own pleasure.

As a child those who should have cared for you violated you. Those who should have protected you ignored you and those who should have loved you betrayed you. Those people whom you relied on took advantage of you.

The important element for the child is whether she thought, or felt, she had a relationship with the abuser. In these circumstance the abuser doesn't need to use force: the power is inherent in the relationship he has.

The abuser may have been a father, mother, step-parent, grandparent, uncle, aunt, priest, teacher, neighbour, older sibling and so on. The most common is father-daughter. It is the relationship with the abuser that is important. If the abuser was someone close to you whom you trusted and looked up to then the effects are devastating. In these circumstances a great deal of pain is felt from not being protected, particularly by your mother.

A child can cope with almost anything provided she is made to feel safe, know that she is OK, is asked what she is feeling, knows she is believed and that the grown-up will do all in their power to stop what is happening.

If after the first time Carole was touched inappropriately her mother had noticed and had said 'I believe you,

---

* Feldmar A (1989) 'Did you used to be R D Laing?' London, Channel Four, Oct 3.

you are not to blame' and had done something to stop the abuse Carole could have grown up thinking and feeling she was OK. Ignoring her distress caused her as much hurt as the sexual abuse itself.

As soon as you were shown dirty pictures, made to watch someone naked or listen to them talking sexually, fondled, forced to masturbate or suck your abusers genitals or were penetrated, your world became in an instant an unsafe place to be. The rules have changed – new ones need to be learned.

Carole's story shows how abuse causes the child to be unable to take delight or joy in any part of her life. No longer can she think about what she will watch on television or wonder what she will get for her birthday – all she can think about is how to avoid being violated again.

The harm was done as soon as the abuser's touch went from harmless cuddling and affection to sexually inappropriate touch or mood. For example, the child notices a change in her father's breathing but does not know what it means, at the same time she feels uncomfortable and senses it is not right. This creates a conflict which she finds difficult to cope with.

Whether the abuse happened once or occurred frequently with father or the man down the road it was still sexual abuse and was severely harmful. The effects are unvarying – the child and her world is never the same again. Abuse is ALWAYS traumatic.

Abuse is rarely a one-off experience; it becomes a part of the child's life and may continue into adulthood. The abuser doesn't always abuse just one child but moves onto others, sometimes abusing several at once.

The abuser may make the child become, in some way, his partner even if he has a wife or girlfriend. As Carole says: 'he used to try and make me ask him for sex – he wanted to pretend he was my boyfriend'. We also know she was made to wear her mother's underwear and sleep in the marital bed when her mother was in hospital.

Everything was turned upside down in the most disturbing and harrowing way. Betrayal is immediate. The child's instinctive trust is destroyed and her body and self invaded.

Her links with the outside world were severed abruptly. If those familiar to her can not be trusted who can be? Everyone and everything became immediately false and she became isolated.

The child may feel numb, confused, disgusted, ashamed, frightened and guilty. This will show in her behaviour. She may begin to wet the bed, have nightmares, withdraw into herself, avoid being at home, do badly at school and much more. This is made all the worse because she isn't allowed to talk about it.

Out of the chaos of the feelings and the disruption of life she has to make sense of it all. She has to discern order so that something is predictable in her life, especially the pain. If she can not, the pain can be unbearable. As Tracy says: 'Mainly it was not knowing that got to me – I would lay awake each night wondering if he was going to come into to my room that night. Usually he did, but it was never regularly so I had no way of knowing – I lived my life in terrifying limbo'

The act of abuse is so separate and different from everything in her life so far and affects every aspect of her waking and sleeping life. The child is forced into a life in which she can not naturally be a child. She can not cuddle, wander around naked or even in her nighty, she can not feel free to have a bath, to sleep in her own bed, to play and to be alone with adults. As Sue says: 'I remember going to my friend's house and she wasn't up. She came rushing downstairs with just her pants on. I was so embarrassed and thought Oh god put some clothes on, you can't do that, your dad is here. She would always be running around in baby doll pyjamas and I thought why can't I do that. I never felt free'.

She has learned the world is a dangerous place, that it is untrustworthy, crazy, unsafe and frightening. She has learned that what she sees is not always what it seems. She lives in fear and anticipation of the abuse happening again.

Fear pervades every fragment of the victim's life. When will he do it again? Will I survive this time? She also lives in fear of her secret being discovered and the abuser executing his threats.

One of the most important aspects of childhood is being like other children whether it is having the same shoes as them, watching the same television programmes or having the same experience. The abused child loses her security of being like everybody else. She looks like others from the outside but feels very different inside.

As Carole says: 'I always felt different. I thought I had been picked out for punishment by my father but I didn't know why that was. I longed to be like other children, with fathers who played normal games with them and who didn't take them to places they didn't like.'

She fears joining in cloakroom gossip or drawing attention to herself in case she reveals her secret. She may become compliant, quiet and detached. She feels dirty, bad and feels no-one could love her.

The child may continue the painful struggle to be accepted by others through minimising her experience or altering it to fit the norm. Others, like Donna, turn to being loners and withdraw from other children. 'I was a loner. I sat on my own and played on my own. I never played with people. I think a lot of abused children get overlooked – nobody notices the child on the outside – nobody looks for it.'

She may turn to overdosing and attempted suicide but still not reveal her pain. She may run away, drink, abuse drugs and end up being labelled deviant or a delinquent.

Feelings of shame, anger, badness, helplessness, powerlessness and guilt are with her throughout the day and at night she fears going to sleep because she relives her experiences through nightmares.

Like Carole, Donna, Sue and the other women in this book you were no different from other children. No more pretty, precocious, vulnerable or stupid.

It is impossible for children to invite sexual acts from adults. They do not have the knowledge or the inclination

The act will always be planned and executed by the adult. The abuser will ALWAYS be responsible for the abuse but the family inadvertently 'sets the scene', by not noticing your needs and feelings; not watching you closely enough; allowing you to be around abusive people; not valuing you by beating you; not believing you; ignoring your silent cries of help and not teaching you how to protect yourself.

The abuse was done to you – it was not done because of you.

The following stories were told by adults but experienced by children.

Tracy

'He masturbated me with a candle he made for me and spied on me in the bathroom with a two way mirror (after ordering me to masturbate). He penetrated me with his fingers and then with his penis. He would make me pretend he was anyone I fancied. He made me watch pornographic videos (containing children at times) and make me stand in front of a sun lamp naked with my sister while he positioned our bodies. He would leave pornographic magazines in my room for me to read. He used to undress me and check me over externally and internally to see if I was ready for a boyfriend. He would suck my nipples for my own good he would say (I was 10 years old!) and, using a child's microscope, check my vaginal secretions. He took photographs of me when I started secondary school and made me show my knickers. He showed his friends. I hated him for this.'

Julia

'When I was 53 I began to retrieve memories of Satanic abuse. They followed on as I recovered memories of incest with my father. At first I remembered that my mother, an aunt and my grandmother had abused me occasionally. Then I remembered my grandfather had exposed himself to me. I found I was drawing pictures of a group of faces with pipes and penises. Then there were devils in the pictures. Then I remembered my granny hitting me after finding me in bed with my father whilst my mother was in hospital having a baby (this was connected to a previous memory). Then I remembered my grandfather took me to places where games were played in which sexual violation of me followed by a group of 8 to 10 men. Gradually I realised that the devils were 'real'. The men dressed in devils costumes – one main devil and several minions. The children also dressed as small devils. We enacted plays about the story of Adam and Eve and the decent of Jesus into hell. These plays are documented in literature about mystery plays in the 10th and 11th century which were taken from secular plays.

Around this time I remembered through drawings that my grandmother had aborted me around the age of 12 or 13. This is when I thought I would bleed to death. I drew a saw, hammers, axes and meat cleavers. I then drew a baby on a bench with a spike being stuck through it with a small picture of a baby being injected through its umbilicus. Suddenly the whole thing came together as happening on a farm with an orchard, a river and woods nearby. I now know this fits the description of my grandmothers brother's farm which we visited often as children, but of which I had no previous recollection. The pictures of devils, fires, running in fear, being raped while tied to a tree or bench, jumping a horsewhip followed by rape have gradually come to form a whole picture of Satanic ritual abuse.

I am aware that these cults use all sorts of tricks and deception to deceive the children they are tormenting, so some of the memories may be distorted, but I know that overall they are true.

My memories are vague but I know my grandfather started by getting me to suck his penis when I was a small baby. It is not hard to imagine how I was coerced. He also said it was to make his 'little man' better or sometimes to show that I loved him. He made me special, his favourite and was always kind and loving by day. My overwhelming feeling was that I must make him better and above all not let him see he was upsetting me in any way. I also had the same feeling about my mother, so it would not have been possible to tell her as she would have been upset. The abuse always happened in the night so I was unable to see him or I kept my eyes shut – or both. Recently I have had pictures of 'steel grey' eyes.

Carol

He used to touch me rubbing, my private parts. He made me touch his penis or he used to lay on top of me moving up and down, but not entering me. He made me put it in my mouth. I fought and kept on fighting.

Sue

I can not remember when the abuse started it must have been when I was about 11. I remember seeing a friend of mine in the summer holidays whom I hadn't seen for a few weeks and her boobs had started to develop, and I thought to myself 'I bet her dad hasn't touched her. What my dad is doing to me has stunted my growth. The abuse seemed to go on forever. I would be sat in the front room and he always sat by the fire. He would make me sit on the pouffe, then start to do things to me I didn't want him to. In my mind I knew it was wrong. I hated him for doing that and as I'm writing this it makes me feel dirty and weird. Sometimes he would follow me upstairs and catch me in the bedroom. Then he would start fingering me and pressing himself against me. This went on for months. I was afraid of being alone with him in the house. Even when I had my periods I wasn't safe – he'd catch me coming out of the bathroom after a bath.

My dad used to do a milkround and I used to have to help. He worked for someone else and they employed me, but I always landed up having to help my dad. In the morning he would come and get me, sometimes playing with my breasts, which used to wake me. I hated that. I can remember him cycling going off to load the van. It would be dark. I would then walk into town to meet him. If we had gone past a certain place I knew it would be OK, I was safe; if not, he'd mess me about. We would invariably park up. It was always secluded and then he would start. I used to sit there and take it – what else could I do? I longed for him to stop and I wished for someone to come along but no-one ever did. He must have known that. He would deliberately not book in the people's milk until we got to this lane, then sit there and do his books, then have a go at me. I used to ask my brother to do it but he'd say 'I'm not getting up yet, it is too early. I hated him for that I really did. I hated both of them. In the end it happened at home a lot – I just wouldn't go home. It didn't matter if people were in the house he would find a way – he'd just sort of catch me. It just stopped happening. I didn't know why but I was glad.

Donna

My life of being abused.

This is what I remember. It started when I was very young. My brother, although he had his own room, always slept in with my sister and me. He gave me lots of cuddles and put his penis between my thighs. I remember it didn't hurt so I didn't really say anything, but at the time I knew it wasn't right. He told me I was special and, like my other brother, said it was our secret.

The next person I remember is an old man who lived in a big house behind ours. I don't know exactly how old I was but I was in school. I can not remember his name. He had a disabled wife who was ill and used to sleep downstairs. My sister and I used to play in the big house. We loved the big rooms and all the old stuff. We went over there for a couple of years.

Nothing happened until his wife died. Then we used to

spend the nights on weekends and at first he just used to snoop around the house. It was fun. Then he started to sleep with us and he made it into a game. We were too young to know how wrong it was and after all it was just another secret to me. He knew exactly how to play it. I can see that now. He used to dare us to touch his penis and tell us how good we were because it was getting bigger. Then he used to get us to suck it, it was awful. He told us if we didn't he would tell our dad we'd touched him. He would play each one of us off against the other and give us money. The more we did the more money he gave us and the greater the dare became. It stopped when our house burned down and we were getting too old to be dared.

When I was about twelve I was feeding my ponies and bedding them down for the night. I went into the small barn and a little time later Darren came in. At first I thought he had come to help me. He was 20 years old and I was always a bit scared of him. He didn't come and help me but pulled a big knife out and told me to lie on the hay and take my pants down. I was so scared I couldn't even scream. I was terrified. All I could do was what he said. Just as he undid his trousers my mum ran through the door. I was so pleased to see her. She ordered me into the house and was screaming at Wayne. The next thing I remember is the that police were asking me all sorts of things. That was the start of two weeks of hell. I had to take two weeks off school and the police blamed me – never mind that I was only twelve. My name was mud. Shortly after that we moved and I changed school. I had to go to high school one year early because they said I didn't fit in with the rest of the girls as I was so advanced in my appearance.

Shortly after that we met Mr and Mrs Margin.* I don't even know how they met my mother. We lived in the country and the nearest house was two miles away. They asked if I could go and live with them for a while as Mrs had to go into hospital and they could use me to help with

* Names have been changed

the house and kids. So I went to stay there. I always liked helping my mum and she needed the money.

I was there about four days when I had a date with my first real boyfriend. He didn't show up so I phoned him and he told me he didn't want to see me again. I was devastated and sat on the sofa crying. Mr Margin came and sat beside me, putting his arms around me and cuddling me in the same way as a father or brother. He said not to worry, that I would have other boyfriends. Then he started to undo my blouse, and when I tried to stop him he told me to behave and that other boys had done it and he would hurt me.

When I tried to get up he held me down and said if I didn't help him he would tell my mother I was bad and didn't do as I was told. She wouldn't get any money which I knew she needed badly. Then he took me to his bedroom and undressed me, and that was the first time I had intercourse. I remember that I didn't hurt much but I just closed my eyes and wished he would hurry up and get off because I felt like he was about to suffocate me – he was heavy. When he finished he sent me to my bed and said I had better come straight back from school or else. Well, this happened every night. I felt powerless. The day his wife came home I remember feeling really relieved. But how wrong I was. I was packing my clothes thinking that I could get out of there and home when she called me into their bedroom and said that her husband needed me to stay. She said that he had a high sex drive and because of her operation she could not have sex for a few days. So she said that I had to stay – they gave me the pill (which made me really sick) and the nightmare began.

She said if I didn't, because first I told her no, that she would tell my mother that while she was in hospital I was sleeping with her husband. I was trapped, so that night when all the kids were asleep (including me — I remember thinking when I went to bed thank god not tonight, but how wrong I was —) she came and woke me up and told me her husband needed me. It was worse than before. When she got me to the bed she told me to undress and I thought she was going to leave but after she got me into bed she got in as well. First he started to touch me and then when he was having intercourse she started to touch my breast then to my horror she tried kissing me I felt really sick. The second night she gave me this really sexy night-gown and then she forced me to touch her. At that time I wished I was dead. I tried many times to run back home, but they would either come to get me or pick me up along the road and drag me into the car. It got so bad they used to meet me straight from school.

I pick one night when I was fighting back. They spiked a glass of coke and I don't know what they put in it, but that night they had me posing for pictures – they were gross. The next morning I woke up in my bed with my own pyjamas on so I didn't know what happened until I said I was going home after school she dragged me into the bedroom and showed me the pictures and said she would show them to everyone. After that I planned and thought I was going to get everything I could out of them. Because my mother couldn't afford a lot of nice things I thought I could get them this way. It worked twice. Great! I finally got out because I met Ian who I married. I was 14½ when I met him. So this went on for a year or more. Even after I met Ian they would meet me from school but I soon learned they wouldn't do anything if Ian was there. Maybe because Ian was 6 years older they couldn't just drag me off the street. So I went home and they tried to make it so that at weekends I went to stay with them, but they soon ran out of excuses and if I could manage it I would tell my mother I didn't want to go. But I had to do it when they weren't there and I used to go and hide if I saw them coming.

Come the end, I told Ian about it. Of course I didn't go into detail, but Ian went with me to see them and as far as I remember my mother didn't know, but I am not sure. Ian had a fight with Mr and Mrs Margin and they left me alone after a while.

The nightmare was over so I just tried to forget. I was scared to tell because I didn't think anyone would listen or do anything because of what the police said when Darren tried to rape me.'

SURVIVAL

'It is about the silence of nights spent holding in screams, holding back tears, holding in one's very self. And it is the stillness of days when all a young girl's resources are used up in keeping the secret from everyone, sometimes even herself.'*

My coping mechanisms – I would imagine he was not there and I was somewhere else. I could block it into darkness and deal with it (cry) later when he wouldn't see me. I would also fix my mind on an object and stare at it, never moving but never fighting back. It was not worth arguing as he would have carried on anyway. It was as though I was two people – I was a child who was being hurt and then I would have to be a grown woman and go along with it. It ended quicker that way. I would go limp and numb. I could feel what was going on, but it would never register until later on and then I would cuddle myself or my teddy, rocking myself and crying. *Tracy*

I can remember I ate quite a lot as a child. I never realised it then, but I do now . It was a comfort and I have thought over the years that if I was fat no-body would want or love me. I started drinking when I was 12 or 13 years old – you can not think when you've been drinking so it helped for a while, or so I thought. *Carol*

I detached myself from everything around me. *Jackie*

I closed my eyes to make everything black. When my eyes were open I stared at the ceiling thinking this isn't really happening. I am not really alive. *Anon*

From the moment the abuse begins the child strives to

* Ellen Bass et al *I never told anyone* 1983 Harper and Row

make sense of it and take some control of the situation. She will behave, think and feel in a way which makes it easier for her to carry on and ultimately survive.

The ways she comes up with are a tribute to her survival as a child – she is creative and inventive. The child will do anything to survive and reduce the feelings of being overwhelmed. Since she can not physically run away she develops other survival methods, with the limited skills she has at her disposal; these soon become habitual.

All children develop ways of coping, but the victim of abuse develops exceptional ways because of her experiences. These children have to turn inward to make sense of their situation; they develop a style of managing, since they can not turn to other people. These methods serve an important function in seeing them through to another day. The quotations above represent just a few methods the child can use.

Like Tracy, many children use disassociation or splitting – they know they can not escape so they detach themselves from what is happening. This may range from mild experiences – shutting off your mind from your body sensations – or it may take the form of having a similar experience to an out-of-the body experience and escaping to somewhere else.

The child may separate her feeling from her thinking; pretend to be asleep; think of other things; recite or sing songs in her head, and thereby blanking out the pain which accompanies the physical suffering. She may split off more than one part of herself – her feelings, behaviour and awareness, anaesthetise her body into not feeling. She never feels whole because a part of her is always closed. She can only deal with a certain amount of pain, so blocking and separation alleviate some of her distress.

The victim may minimise her experience, saying 'It isn't that bad, at least he doesn't . . .', or 'all dads do this,' or she may deny it completely. She may rationalise it by saying 'daddy did it because . . . ,' always making up reasons for it to be happening.

Some children pretend it never happened.

Denial gives the child a breathing space. If she denies the reality of abuse to herself she also denies the pain which accompanies it. She can then proceed with what she has to do in her everyday life – go to school, carry out her homework, attend family gatherings – right down to to keeping herself clean, eating and so on.

Denial is protective because it safeguards the child from something she can not yet face – she protects herself by not remembering.

If she enters denial she will not have to admit that her parents are bad or that possibly she is bad. To outsiders she denies the truth because it helps her survive – literally.

Denial is common in the abusive family, it is a successful way of avoiding the truth and guarding secrets. The abuser invariably denies the reality or at least attempts to justify his actions: 'it was for her own good'.

Even though Carole could remember a lot of her experience, she had still blocked or repressed parts of it. She was protecting herself from the enormity of the pain. Other women can not remember parts of their experience and some remember nothing. Some may remember the details of the abuse but not attach any sense of feeling to it – the child blocks the feelings because they were too painful. The survivor may talk in depth about what happened but not show any emotion. When asked what she feels she may say 'I think I feel . . .' or simply 'I don't know.' Carole said 'I do not think about my body.'

When the abuse occurred those around probably acted as if nothing out of the ordinary was happening. Even when the abuse happened in the room next to where the rest of the family were, perhaps no-one noticed – even though they may have heard your cries and seen the evidence of your distress. This denial causes the victim to question the reality of her situation. To stop herself from feeling crazy she had to suppress the memories.

Denial, splitting and disassociation are ways in which the child survives her abusive situation, by moving her experiences out of her conscious awareness until a time when she is better able to deal with the reality.

She may turn to fantasy. As Tracy says: 'I found it good to have a fantasy world where you were liked and everyone you met was a friend' and 'I never saw my mum for who she really was – it was as though I saw her as I wanted her to be, a perfect mum'. Other children may fantasise that abuser is separate from her father, brother or uncle and create a person who is loving and kind, and who does not do things to her.

She may fantasise about venting her feelings, killing the abuser or running away from home, or that she is someone different – a person from television, for example. She may create fantasy figures to cope with her awful family or she may fantasise into the future.

Carole fantasised and coped by believing that one day the abuse would stop – it helped her through each day. She says: 'When I was a child I never considered suicide because I always had the strong hope that the abuse would end.' Little did she know it would last ten years; if she had, perhaps her coping mechanism would not have worked.

The child may avoid bad feelings by turning to books or television as a way of coping. As Sue says 'I used to escape into books'.

Some survivors cope by 'creating' arguments and friction in the family. Sue says: 'I was aggressive and bad tempered and we rowed a lot'. This is one way of releasing the rage and keeping the family secret.

The child may become highly-alert, constantly aware of family members' whereabouts and activities, so preparing herself for the abuse, always trying to protect herself from another attack. She may take every opportunity to escape the abuse, so that her life is guided by avoiding it. She may not go into certain rooms or do certain things which put her at risk.

The child may harm herself by cutting or burning herself, so that she can centre her mind on that pain rather than the pain of her feelings. She may become obsessively tidy and ordered, to create a sense of control over her life.

She may take on the responsibility for the abuse so she

feels in control of it by feeling guilty. Feeling guilty feels better than having no control at all, and also has the effect of rationalising and making sense of it all.

Like Carol, the child may have turned to drink or food as a way to escape her feelings – taking charge of her eating, either through bulimia or anorexia, is one way of coping and taking control. Being overweight is a way of protecting herself from people ('if I am overweight nobody will want me'). She may make herself look ugly, unattractive or masculine to try to keep safe.

The child may become an over-achiever in many aspects of her life – work, motherhood, as a wife and so on.

Sadly, when the torment is too great for the child she may suffer mental illness or may even try to kill herself. She may create solutions to problems which appear insurmountable by deciding that if things become really bad she can always kill herself, hurt others or go crazy (end up in a mortuary, prison or asylum). This is a way of protecting herself from feeling the pain and moving through it. These are known as 'escape hatches' and 'are decided upon in early life to be exercised when life got too stressful'.*

Carole says: 'I remember hoping I would go crazy or get ill to escape the nightmare my life had become.'

Even though Carole did not use suicide as a way out of her situation she did attempt to put herself in hospital. She says: 'I didn't want to kill myself but hurt myself enough to have to go into hospital or stay in bed so I would be 'unavailable' to my father. On one particularly bad day he made me get into the van he used for work. He was in a very bad temper because I wouldn't cooperate with his wishes, and he drove into the country at night. I was really frightened – I had no idea where we were going or what he was going to do. We were travelling quite fast and I opened the door to jump out but he saw it and dragged me back, making him even angrier. He stopped

* Holloway W H (1973). 'Shut the Escape Hatch,' in the Monograph Series Number I–X. Ohio Midwest Institute for Human Understanding Inc.

the van in a gateway and made me get out. He wanted to take me into a field but I didn't want to go. He told me to climb over the gate, and when I wouldn't he picked me up by my clothes, opened the gate and dragged me through it. I fell down and passed out, not with suicide in mind but in a desperate attempt to stop what was happening'.

Later in life Carole decided that if things became too bad she could always kill herself, which, like other women, did not necessarily mean using overt methods. 'When I was having a difficult time in my marriage, I overdosed on alcohol. I was staying with a friend at the time, and she asked me what was wrong, so I told her what I had done. I was taken to hospital to have my stomach pumped. I haven't made any other suicide attempts but the thought has crossed my mind many times. I remember going to a chemist to buy some tablets during my time with the therapy group, but it was closed. That was enough to make me think again. Sometimes life just doesn't seem worth the hassle, which seems strange because I didn't think that when the awful things were happening to me.'

The child has few resources to draw on and, in her immature way, copes as best she can. Her behaviour is not abnormal but normal in response to her plight. She used the solutions of a five, six or seven- year- old, which are hard pressed to cope with normal adult demands. Some of these coping skills will be useful to her as an adult but some will prevent her from having a fulfilled life.

Healing is about changing patterns of coping and making them more appropriate. Above all, once she is an adult the child has to forgive herself for the ways she coped and not to blame herself. She has to honour what she did to survive and stroke herself for keeping intact – even if she feels she has only just managed to.

If the denial is strong the child and adult must realise she is protecting something important, and when she is ready she will be able to face what she needs to cloak at present.

WHY DIDN'T THE CHILD TELL?

I just did as I was told – he was my father. *Sue*

He said I was 'special' and I stopped getting into trouble. He never seemed to have time for us kids. *Carol*

I never said anything because it never hurt me and they both said it was our secret. *Donna*

He kept me silent by threatening 'bruises that wouldn't show' and saying my mum wouldn't believe me or want me. *Tracy*

It would have been pointless to tell mum. Her response to my problems were always tears about how it made her feel (even if it was just a cut knee!). *Julia*

I was told no-one would like me and no-one would believe me. *Anon*

'compliance can not be equated with complicity in the abuse'*

It was essential for the abuser to prevent you from telling. He had to silence you, his victim, to keep you powerless and for the abuse to continue.

The fact that the abuser was an adult and you are a child means he already had a position of power and trust from which he could decide what happens.

He knew there was no way you could stop him doing what he wanted because you lacked the physical strength, developed intellect, emotional security to go against his wishes. You had no choice – you were taught to obey.

Poignantly every child is aware that she relies on her

* Liz Hall and Siobhan Lloyd *Surviving Child Sexual Abuse* A handbook for helping women challenge their past, The Falmer Press, 1989, p. 111.

parents and the greatest threat to her is abandonment.
Probably all she knows of life is through her family, so the
threat of abandonment underpins why she doesn't tell.
She is justifiably afraid. She learns not to rock the boat
because it is easier and safer. She enters the denial of the
family.

The abuser uses his power in many ways to keep his
victim from telling.

Depending on which methods he uses he plays on
different feelings – fear, guilt, love and confusion.

If he threatens a child with 'If you tell I will . . .' she
believes him. Her experience is that adults have the power
to make things happen, or not.

As Carole was aware there is no greater authority than
father. Carole's father threatened to kill her. He was a
violent man and she had seen what he was capable of. She
had witnessed him using his power over his wife and
mother and they didn't, or couldn't, stop him. She had no
doubt that she couldn't have done anything different or
that his were not empty threats.

As Jacqueline Spring says in 'Cry Hard and Swim' 'To
live in such a household is like travelling in a car being
driven by an insane driver. We are cut off from any pass-
ing help. We know that if we cry out from the window he
will simply speed up and kill us. He has told us so, and
everything we know about him, about the world we live
in, confirms it'.

Carole would frequently know the force of her father's
fury and violence. The messages he gave her about not
telling and keeping his secret were made all the more
potent because of his size and brutality. As one writer says
when the threat 'is made by a witch or giant whose
features are distorted with rage, whose voice smashes
through all defences of the child's mind, and whose hand
is ever ready to strike humiliation and terror into his face
and head' it is all the more forceful and impossible to go
against.

The abuser may use other threats. He may warn that if
he goes to prison the family will break up and the child

will be sent away. He may say her mother will be very upset. He will tell the child everyone will stop loving her. Thus, the child carries the intolerable burden of feeling responsible for the family's future.

He may threaten her with punishment. In Carole's case, 'the punishment I received for not co-operating with the abuse was being beaten, deprived of sleep, given no peace and never left alone.'

Though Carole's Sunday school teacher knew something was wrong, Carole could not tell him because she was too afraid. 'I didn't need to tell him – he knew – but he couldn't help at first because I wouldn't admit it. I had to pretend nothing was wrong in front of other people. Fear, shame, embarrassment and guilt stopped me from telling.'

Later when Carole was an adult she was still afraid to tell the family secret, such was the influence and control of her father. Many times in her therapy we would see evidence of his power and the importance of secrecy. Each time she spoke of the horror of her childhood her hand would rise involuntarily to her mouth or throat and her voice would soften, symbolic of her fear of telling. Breaking her father's prohibition was one of the most formidable and painful aspects of her healing.

The abuser may have already set the child up to fear she has collaborated in some way by saying: 'I know you'd always want to please Daddy', or by making her body respond naturally to his touch. He makes her responsible in some way by saying 'I wouldn't have done it unless you wanted me to' or 'If you said no I would have stopped'. He may say 'No-one will believe you'.

Sexual abuse can be gentle and affectionate and the child comes to have faith in believing it is love and affection; her body responds naturally to this touch.* It is normal for a childs body to become sexually aroused, just

---

* The child's body may become sexually aroused but she can not understand this as an adult would. The event does not hold any meaning for her because it does not form part of an adult relationship.

as if she is tickled she will laugh. The abuser may use this against her by saying, or implying that she wanted sexual touch, she enjoyed it. She can not know her body is capable of having an orgasm, so she concludes in her childlike way that she is responsible. She feels she has betrayed herself , but she is always innocent.

The abuse may be the only way the child receives attention and a feeling that she is needed or the abuser may be the only person who cares for the child. She does not want the sexual touch but wants and needs the attention. She feels bad for receiving attention in this way, but the abuser will then only give her attention in this way.

Children are easy targets; they can easily feel they are responsible for their parents' behaviour. It is often easier for a child to blame herself than be critical of her parents. The absence of self-blame in the child is unusual, as she is driven to perceive the reasons for the maltreatment to be within herself. The abuser makes the child feel guilty and responsible for his sexual arousal and the situation: 'Look what you have made me do'.

He uses her guilt to perpetuate his vicious cycle of abuse. After not telling the first time, because she knows she can not, she feels guilty because she believes, falsely, she has become a collaborator. He knows this and uses her belief to continue the abuse. As Donna says: 'She said if I didn't stay she would tell my mother I had been sleeping with her husband while she was in hospital'.

Often, feeling guilty and in some way to blame is the child's way of gaining and feeling in control. As one writer says: 'This illusion of power seems better than acknowledging one has no power at all'.*

A child desperately needs love from adults. The abuser will define the abuse as love, saying 'I love you' or 'I'm going to teach you about love and sex' or 'this is what people do when they love each other'. He will also challenge the child's love and devotion for him with such

* Linda Sanford *Strong At The Broken Places*, Virago, 1991, p. 43.

phrases as 'if you really loved me you would let me do this, not make a fuss,' making her feel compelled to follow his wishes.

The abuser tells innumerable lies to cover up his actions, convincing himself and the child their's is a loving relationship and he is not to blame. The child wants to believe this. She will see bribes as tokens of love and he reinforces this by treating her as 'special'. He will play on the fact that the abuse may be the only way the child receives love and attention.

Only as she grows older does the child develop the ability to understand that this is not the case which, in turn, leads her to feel guilty and ashamed.

In Donna's case: 'My brothers, especially the oldest, told me I was special. There was no way I was going to jeopardise that, because they and my dad were the only ones who said it. I didn't get it from my mum, she didn't tell me that'.

The abuser typically discounts his actions and convinces himself the child was willing. He tells her it is all right and it happens to all children. She is left feeling bewildered. As one writer says 'When the child recovers from such an attack, (s)he feels enormously confused, in fact, split – innocent and culpable at the same time – and *her* confidence in the testimony of *her* own senses is broken.'*

He may even start the abuse before she can talk, so she grows up feeling or thinking it is normal. Later, she may feel confused, knowing it is wrong but not having the words to express herself she may only be able to say 'Dad is being horrible to me again'. She knows it feels bad and will always doubt herself before doubting her parent. He imposes his beliefs on her, leaving her confused and feeling crazy. She attributes the cause to herself or chastises herself for thinking anything is wrong. She can not

*From International Psychoanalyticcal Library 1955 48 'Final Contributions to the Problems and Methods of Psychoanalysis' S. Ferenczi, Hogarth Press Ch. – 'Confusion of Tongues Between the Adult and the Child', 1933.

trust her own judgement. The abuser also tells her 'this is what all daddies/uncles/brothers do', further emphasising her lack of judgement.

She may believe that 'If something is wrong then my mother or another adult would stop it.' Children often see mother, aunts, grandmothers as being larger and capable of doing things the child can not. She comes to believe adults will not be available to her when she is in need of help.

Carole's mother and grandmother may not have been consciously aware of the abuse (to begin with) but they ALLOWED it to continue. A child in this position may think nothing is wrong, because her mother lets it continue, but at the same time she FEELS something is wrong. As one woman says 'It didn't feel OK but who was I to question mum and dad?'. Her internal reality does not match her external one, which makes her feel crazy or, at least, confused.

This was another woman's experience: 'At first I thought it was normal, so I talked about it to my friends in a subtle way, as Dad told me not to tell anyone. It was when other people did not want to know me because I was 'strange' I realised it wasn't normal, so I kept quiet. No one ever told an adult about it so I was never helped.'

In many abusive families the child feels she is not important; she does not tell because she feels no-one cares enough about her. The child desperately wants to make herself lovable and valuable to her parents. She often feels greater despair when, after doing everything she can, the abuse continues. She has not been successful, even her parents do not love her enough.

For Julia, enduring the abuse was an attempt at pleasing her family, she says. 'I said to myself "it doesn't matter I don't matter". I felt that I must always be helpful to others. I was always being 'good' and hoping that they might love me if I did this for them. I realised that I was starved of real love and thought this a means of being loved.'

For the child, if she has any role or importance, it is the role of providing for her parents' needs: to provide her father with sexual gratification, her mother with protection from the truth, and the rest of her family and herself with protection from her father's anger should she refuse to comply with his wishes.

She may feel guilty about talking about family problems to outsiders or extended family members and is compelled to try to remedy the troubles within the family. As one writer says: 'Children have the compulsion to put to rights disorder in the family, to burden, so to speak, their own tender shoulders with the load of all the others. Of course this is not only out of pure altruism, but is in order to be able to enjoy again the lost rest and the care and attention accompanying it.'* But she is always fighting a losing battle – a child can never cure a families ills.

If the abuse happens outside her family she knows from the family rules and experience of how the family 'works' that she can not tell. Donna says: 'My sister is a year younger than me, but she was always the smart one and knew best, so if I said anything and he had said it hadn't happened my mother would most likely have believed her and I would have got the blame for lying. And when she did ask, I had to say no because my sister didn't say anything. Come to think about it, my sister and I never talked about it at all.'

Even though Donna 'knew' her sister had also been abused she could not tell her about her own experience. She says 'She asked me once if one of my brothers had ever touched me. I said: 'no'.' To say yes would have gone against the family's commands.

The 'abusive' families run on denial – they don't know what you see, don't know what you hear and don't know what you feel. The family does not acknowledge what is going on, which is why in Sue's family her father could abuse her while other family members were in the house. Sue says: 'It happened at home a lot and in the end it didn't matter if there were any people in the house. He would find a way – he would just sort of catch me.'

* Ferenczi – 1933.

Children abused by people outside the close family group may still not tell. It is the make-up of the family which prevents them from feeling they are able to tell. The family is not well-adjusted. In the event of abuse in the 'good enough' family the child would feel able to tell AND mother or father would notice something was wrong.

Poignantly, one woman, on being asked why didn't she tell, replied 'No-one ever asked'.

Carole

My father rarely let me out of his sight. I was allowed to go to work and to the chapel, where I think he thought he could trust me not to get involved with anyone. Like school, work was my refuge from my terrible life at home. I have generally got on well with my colleagues bit I wasn't encouraged to have friends in fact It was actively discouraged, particularly with the opposite sex. I used to meet Gordon sometimes in my lunch hour if my father was out of town on business. Gordon knew I was in a bad way and told me to contact him at any time if I needed him. That offer was my hope and my safety – I knew I could trust him and eventually I told him everything. At no time did he even consider backing out or letting me down. He was there for ME, something I had never experienced before.

That was my first disclosure. Gordon believed me. I know the fear of not being believed is one of the reasons many abused children do not disclose, so I consider myself fortunate to have had Gordon to turn to. It was not difficult, because I was simply confirming something he already knew. Once I had actually put it into words the rest was easy, because it was Gordon, and my trust in him was so strong. I should have done it before, because he would always have been there. I knew he loved me enough for that.

Gordon went to the police the same day – court was a nightmare My father was sitting opposite me and his eyes bore through me. Expressing myself was not at all easy; I just didn't have the words then. 'Sexual abuse' was not a phrase often heard in 1957, but I had Gordon's support – he was there and the police were wonderful. I do not know what Gordon said to them but I was never made to feel my story was in any doubt.

I was taken to a clinic to be examined internally, which was a painful experience. After that I was sent to a home for 'naughty girls' and felt very alone. I was told I was there for care and protection, but I was treated exactly the same as the rest and expected to do my share of the work. I didn't mind that, and it was better and safer than going home. There just wasn't anywhere else to put me. I was questioned by the head of home about whether my mother had known what had been going on, and then, and for many years, I believed she couldn't have possibly known. It was only in therapy that I fully accepted the truth. She HAD known and she had ignored it. She wouldn't, or couldn't, protect me or stop it because she was too frightened herself. I can not forgive her for that but I can understand it – her fears was as great as mine.

My mother visited me in the home, but only to question me about Gordon's involvement. She was unable to comfort me in any way even then. Her instructions from my father were to find out as much as she could, nothing else. There was no support from any of the family except my aunt and uncle: they were good to me when I moved to Southsea after the court case. While my father was in prison he forbade mother to have anything to do with me. I received a letter in my mother's handwriting while I was living at the hostel in Southsea, but it was written in my father's words. She said she didn't love me and never wanted to see me again, and told me never to contact her. He had apparently stood over her and dictated every word. I was absolutely devastated – I had only recently arrived in Southsea, alone with only an address to find and two pounds and ten shillings. To receive that letter then seemed like the end of the world.

My father was allowed to return home when he was released from prison. He was given two years imprisonment, of which he served about 13 months. On his return he asked to see me, and I went and I don't know why, except that I was so afraid of him. He showed no remorse at all and blamed me for him being jailed. He said 'being in prison wasn't very nice you know' and I immediately felt guilty – he was so powerful even then. I was frightened of him from a distance, frightened of his power over me and my life. That fear lasted almost 35 years.

My grandmother never forgave me for 'putting him in prison'. He was her favourite son and she made me feel guilty. Even when I was married I obeyed him. He used to work in a shop then, across the street from our flat, and every Saturday he invited himself over for lunch. I didn't want him there but I was afraid to say so. It didn't occur to me that I had a choice. Why should it? – I had never had choices before. The past was never brought up – still secret, always ignored, the status quo preserved.

WHEN THE CHILD TELLS

Those victims who do tell are often faced with a mother who colludes with the abuser, who tells her she is making it up, who tells her to forget it. This makes the child feel guilty and isolated from her family or the outside world from which she has been cut off. She learns to keep quiet for fear of turning more people away from her, and she learns how to please other people.

As one woman says 'When I found the two way mirror behind a cupboard in the toilet I felt I couldn't take any more, and I broke down to mum and told her everything. I wanted help and love from a proper family, but all I received was a confrontation with Mum and Dad. She believed him when he said he was doing it for my own good. It was forgotten. I was hurt. I needed something, but I did not know what. Dad denied any form of penetration and said to me later 'I couldn't admit to that, could I?'.

More often than not the child who tells encounters denial, scepticism and dismissal.

Those mothers who suspect something often do not confront the abuser or support the daughter because they too are entangled in the web of denial, dependency and secrecy. Carol says: 'My mother made me lie to the police to cover for my father, which I did. She begged me to lie because she couldn't cope on her own. My sister was only little and my mother said 'think of your little sister'. The hardest part came a few years ago when my sister told me he did it to her too.'

If she does tell, she may activate a series of events which are as difficult or, in some cases, more threatening and more troubled than the abuse. Father may go to prison, threaten suicide or react with extreme violence. The family may be separated, the perpetrator losing his job, so creating financial insecurity for the family. The victim may be cut off and rejected by her family. If mum chooses to allow the abuser to stay at home, then the victim may have to go into care. Her siblings and wider family may blame her calling her wicked, mad, a liar and accuse her of making up stories. People outside the family may react by taking reprisals, isolating the members, especially the victim.

The disclosure immediately causes great disruption to the family and they are thrown into crisis. The image the family has created themselves and others is dismantled. The carefully preserved secret has been revealed and jeopardises the structure, roles and rules of the family. The family, not only the abuser, generally puts all its efforts into rebuilding the status quo. Change is avoided at all costs.

It is frequently the case that the victim is rejected and is punished. She may be sent away like Carol, who was sent to her grandparents, or Carole, who was sent to a 'naughty girls' school. The family quickly tightens its boundaries, shutting the discloser out or pulling her back into the pathology of the family. In Carole's case she even visited her father in prison, such was the denial and domination of her family.

The victim often feels and in reality is punished. Even when the family are faced with the facts of the abuse they may continue to blame her.

In other families the abuser, once the discloser has been turned out from the family, abuses other children.

When her family has betrayed her, through denial or minimising her needs, the child feels humiliated and shamed. It is difficult to admit that your family has humiliated, violated or betrayed you. Telling highlights her insignificance, so she buries or 'forgets' the experience If she has tried telling and nothing has happened, it reinforces her belief that she is insignificant and unimportant. Even if she has tried to tell, she may not try again, even in adulthood, because of the repercussions experienced as a child.

All children 'tell' in some way, even if they are not aware of it at the time.

As a child, Carole didn't realise that her bed-wetting, which continued until she was eight, was her way of disclosing that something bad was happening to her. She says 'I had always wet the bed but I didn't in hospital, I stopped completely. It seemed like progress to me, that things were getting better, because I had always been made to feel I was naughty when I wet the bed. I hoped other parts of my life would improve, too, that perhaps when I went home my father wouldn't abuse me any more.' The abuse and the bed-wetting were seen as separate. Carole had no way of knowing it was her way of telling and an indication of the immense trauma she was having to face alone. Carole also 'told' by 'having nightmares and screaming when I knew I was going to be left alone with him'.

And Donna says: 'When I was 13 or 14 I used to suffer a lot of thrush and kidney infections . When I was abused by the couple my kidney infections were non-stop and I was forever visiting the doctor. I had thrush from that time until just recently.'

And for Sue 'I was at Senior school and I remember crying when it came to weekends and the holidays. Every one thought I was completely mad but I loved school and hated my home. At school I felt safe.' During Sue's healing she spent time thinking back about the silent ways in which she had tried to tell.

Sue says: 'I wanted to be anywhere but home; I hated it. I didn't like being in the house alone with him and felt such a relief when he went out. I would wait outside Mum's workplace so we could go home together. I became sulky and miserable – really miserable. At school I would cling to a teacher, I hated weekends and school holidays and would cry at the end of term. I didn't like being kissed by relatives when saying 'goodbye'. I would always hang back hoping they would forget me. I always wanted to be clean and couldn't stand dirty hands, I was always washing my body and had to wear clean clothes.'

For Julia 'I had a recurrent nightmare which I know was related to the abuse. I cried everyday when I went to

Junior school – no-one ever asked why, or if they did I made up an excuse like forgetting my dinner money. I tried to be nice to people all the time so they would be kind to me. I hit my younger brother and sister when I was left to baby-sit. I desperately sought affection and was always being good – too good to be true.'

She also says: 'As a child I had pneumonia when staying alone with my grandparents. Later as an adult, when writing about the abuse and just before I developed bronchitis, I had written in my journal 'I am ill granny, I can not go out with grandpa today'.

Donna says: 'I was terrified of old people – it was so obvious. If an old person walked down the street towards me I would cross, but I wouldn't JUST cross – I would run, even if I was with my mum. If an old person was crippled in any way I was petrified, I just froze. Even my grandmother, I wouldn't go near her. My mother took me to the doctor because she couldn't take me anywhere. The doctor told her I was scared of growing old, instead of saying something must have happened to me. I was eight years old.'

Donna also says: 'as a child I was a loner. I sat on my own and played on my own.'

Another woman said she 'disclosed' through 'withdrawal into self and deterioration in my school work' and, another said, 'I was forever saying I hated my dad and I knew too much sexually when it came to boyfriends, but I don't think I led anyone to believe anything was wrong.'

A child may disclose through art or through photographs of her family. As an adult she may clearly see that as a child she did not want to be photographed next to her father or that he is touching her inappropriately in the picture. Photographs of survivors as children often show them looking sad and as though they were carrying the world's troubles on their shoulders.

It is highly unusual in families other than the 'good enough' for these covert ways of telling to be understood. They are more likely to be picked up and labelled, which takes the focus away from the family, making the child the problem rather than the family and abuser. The child becomes the scapegoat and is blamed for the family's troubles. One of Sue's silent ways of telling was to be aggressive towards her father. She says 'I really hated him when I was at home and one night he bashed a hole in my bedroom door after we had rowed – it was awful. Mum was angry and upset with me. She asked what I had done to upset my father. If only she had known, or did she, I wonder?'. The victim becomes the wrong-doer in the eyes of her family.

All the child's effort goes into keeping the family's secret and trying to cope with what is happening to her. The price of secrecy is dear.

HOW ABUSE AFFECTS THE GROWING CHILD

'the real damage of incest, the pain of never being able to accept that someone you loved, looked up to, trusted implicitly, could so casually trample all over you, body and soul, but secretly, and then escape, leaving a false trail of extravagantly generous gestures of fatherhood to conceal the deed'.*

As children we all move through developmental stages of emotional, intellectual and physical growth. Each stage carries new tasks, challenges and liberty for growth, preparing us for later life.

Carole was prevented from moving freely through these stages because the abuse became the focus of her life. She spent her time and energy avoiding it, coping with it, living with it and attempting to survive it.

Experiencing abuse prevents these developmental stages from providing adequately the foundation for our adult life. If our needs are not met and our problems are left unresolved we will carry with us a glut of unfinished

* *Cry Hard and Swim*, J Spring, Virago, 1987, p. 157.

business which will distort our capacity for a healthy contented life and add to any difficulties experienced when we are older.

It is parents who hold the key to their child moving favourably through each stage. Your parents had greater power in EVERYTHING. Physically they were bigger, stronger, more agile, and intellectually they had different, more advanced ways of thinking.

Children have their own way of thinking. Only gradually do they learn to think in the way adults take for granted. Small children's thinking is illogical. The world only consists of their immediate experience, they have no access to other perspectives. They can not make comparisons and think their world is all there is and that everyone in their world has access to their experiences. They have little reference to the outside world beyond their family. This is particularly so for the abusive family who keep themselves isolated from other people.

When the young child is faced with a situation for which she can not find an explanation she assumes: 'This must have something to do with me'. This 'magical thinking', based on her sense of omnipotence, may cause her to 'assume responsibility for an extraordinary range of unhappy events.' As one author writes, for example, if there is a death in her family she takes on the blame of being the murderer.*

It is very easy for parents to reinforce a child's magical thinking or even foster it. The child shows a remarkable capacity for complying with her parents' wishes. To overcome the effects of her immature thinking she needs healthy modelling and reassurance from her parents which shows her she is not to blame or, if daddy is angry, it isn't because she has done something to make him angry. Without adequate information and explanation she will often believe she is the cause of bad feeling.

'Children are not born with standards for evaluating behaviour, social skills or moral values. They learn what

* Bloch D 1979 *So the Witch won't eat me?* London Burnett Books

they see and they do not learn what they do not see.'* As Tracy says, 'I used to think it was normal and no big deal', and for Sue 'I thought it happened to all girls my age'.

A child makes assumptions based on what she is told and what she experiences. If your parents, or other important people said you were bad you would believe it because you didn't know how to challenge them and think logically. You did not know any better.

When Carole was abused at the age of six she intuitively knew it was wrong, but didn't have the ability or power to challenge it. She already understood the rules of her family one of which was to keep quiet and to keep dad happy. Her child perspective was 'I thought it would bring peace for everyone, this is horrible I don't like it, but I've got to do it or life will be hell'.

When the abuse is supported by threats and physical pain, which is often the case, the child has no way of knowing these are only threats, so she complies – she is terrified. A young child believes it when her father says he will kill her, and obeys when her mother says 'Don't tell'. She does not have the abilities to work out how to protect herself, i.e. by telling a person in authority, even if they ask her what is wrong. Her parents appear as all-powerful and omnipotent. Carole says: 'I was threatened with violence and possible death if I told anyone'.

She would have had to break free from everything she had been taught and run the very real risk to herself of being abandoned or killed.

Throughout the stages we pass through we are prepared, or not, for healthy, fulfilling relationships with others AND ourselves. We learn from our parents that we are deserving, we are OK, and important, and if we don't learn this we can not think, behave and feel as if we are.

---

* Jael Greeleaf 'Co-Alcoholic Para-Alcoholic Who's who and what's the difference (Paper presented at the National Council on Alcoholism 1981 Annual Alcoholism Forum New Orleans quoted page 125 in M Utain and B Oliver 'Scream Louder: Through Hell and Healing with an incest survivor and her Therapist' 1989 Health Communications Inc.

We don't have the means to create an accurate picture of ourselves, so we rely on other peoples' reactions.

In the 'good enough' family, where parents make mistakes but essentially do their best for their offspring, the child grows through the various stages and sees the world as an exciting place to be explored. Every situation is greeted with curiosity and wonder. The child is curious and intuitive, and has a 'love affair' with the world.* She plays, she can be intimate and she is spontaneous. She can experience true joy.

She was born with the ability to experience all emotions and, after a period of imitating her parents, develops an ability to distinguish feelings from one another. Her parents respond to her feelings and she feels validated and knows she is OK (even if she isn't perfect).

For the child in the 'abusive' family the world is a scary place where new situations are treated with fear and trepidation. She begins to doubt her intuition and begins not to trust her feelings. She loses her ability to be close to people, for fear of spilling the secrets. In fact she is often not allowed to mix with others. She may becomes calculating and watchful.

She can not develop healthy, protective measures because she is never allowed to explore, play and be spontaneous. She only learns to adapt to what her family require of her. Love is conditional – and if there is no love, then attention is conditional. She is never taught how to look after herself, so she figures it out for herself.

In the 'good enough' family she learns about boundaries, rules and how to protect herself, all within the safety of her parents' home. She makes sense of her environment, and listens and watches attentively, dealing with events as they arise. Her family is consistent, answering questions with answers she can put to the test at a later stage. She learns that her parents and the world are predictable. She develops trust and is secure in the knowledge that whatever happens she will survive.

* Margaret Mahler

In Carole's experience she had to adjust to a system in which lies were promoted above all else and truth was denied; she adhered to her family's rules because she had to survive. She was overwhelmed by fear and helplessness. Instead of consistency and security she had to contend with a childhood of fear, of trying to sort things out for herself.

She feared getting it wrong, feared her father's advances and feared expressing her own feelings. The continual warping of reality through secrecy and her mother and grandmother's denial caused her to feel crazy, rather like being faced with a rampaging lion and then being asked 'What lion?'. She couldn't know what reality was because her family existed through denial.

Without making her feel responsible for problems the 'good enough' parents tell the child what is happening, to keep her from creating fantasies. She can relax, secure in the knowledge that her parents will take care of her.

She develops self-esteem and knows she will be cared for. She runs to her parents if things go wrong, knowing they will comfort her if she cries, protect her if she is scared, repair her wounds if she is hurt and laugh with her if she is happy. She is allowed to know and ask for what she needs.

Having someone use their power over you, particularly someone you trust, to gain sexual pleasure leads to a poor or distorted sense of self. Through actions and words you were told what kind of person you were, and because you were highly vulnerable and receptive to the power of others at this age you accepted this false reality of yourself – because you HAD to. Through the abuse and violence the abuser is giving the child powerful messages about the kind of world she lives in and who she is and the child will make decisions based on these messages.

Carole developed a false self – the Carole others wanted her to be or told her she was, either by overt or covert messages. She believed her feelings, needs and perceptions were all wrong because they were ignored.

She could not know who her 'self' was because she was

not allowed to make her own decisions and was under the total physical and psychological control of her father. She says 'I was never allowed to make decisions of my own; I always had to ask for permission. For some reason I always expected to be treated badly, there was a kind of safety in it.'

In the 'good enough' family the child's parents allow her to take risks so she can learn the consequences of her behaviour. Allowing her do this within the safety of her families rules, boundaries, and permissions she concludes that not everything goes well all the time, but that there are people there to guide and help her.

The 'good enough' family allows her to come and go, nurturing her when she needs it, and allows her to create bonds outside the family. She begins to understand her role in the family and those of other family members.

Carole's family did not provide the safety or freedom for her to move outside the household. In incestuous families the members 'bind themselves together with ropes of mutual dependence, fear of separation, and secrecy, and if any one member tries to break away the bonds are ruthlessly tightened.'* The very small amount of independence Carole was allowed was constantly taken away as a way of controlling her and keeping her in the abusive situation. 'Punishment took the form of being smacked, or deprived of freedom; not being allowed to go out to play or to the church group which I loved, or to listen to my favourite radio programmes.'

Tight boundaries prevented her from seeking the help and guidance she desperately needed from outside the family. Carole says: 'I felt overpowered, controlled, but at the same time abandoned, unprotected and sacrificed for the sake of peace in the everyday lives of the rest of the family'.

Although there are very tight boundaries on the outside of the family the boundaries inside are blurred, so

---

* Eric Berne *Transactional Analysis in Psychotherapy* Grove Press New York 1961, 1966.

that the family members' roles become distorted. Carole says:'He tried to make me ask him for sex, kept me up all night once or twice because I wouldn't; he wanted to pretend that he was my boyfriend' and when her mother went into hospital to have her sister he made Carole take on the role of his sexual partner and wife. He made her sleep in her parents bed for the whole time his wife was in hospital.

Within the boundaries of this family the child is not given space which she can call her own and is not allowed privacy, either physical or psychological. She does not learn that her body or mind belong to her.

The child in the 'good enough' family is allowed to express her true feelings, label them and still receive attention and approval. She is allowed to let people know when she is angry, sad or scared, and she takes this ability into adulthood. She is allowed to think and feel for herself.

In the 'abusive' family ALL the child's effort goes into survival which leaves little time for natural development. She has, to grow up fast, because she has been exposed to experiences far beyond her level of maturity. 'At junior school I remember girls discussing babies and the different ideas they had, some of them quite laughable, and I just stood back thinking 'you know nothing about it at all. What you're saying isn't true, I know what's true', but I didn't want them to know, so I said nothing. Again I felt different from the rest.'

Like other victims Carole's childhood life was organised totally around surviving and coping with the abuse. She had little time for normal childhood activities and feelings because all the time she was trying to think up ways to survive and escape the abuse. 'I tried to persuade my sister or brother to sleep with me, to cuddle right up to me, so that to get me up at night he would have to disturb them which might put him off. It didn't. I used to avoid if possible being in any room alone with him. That's why I dreaded having baths.'

One way of surviving was to ignore her own feelings

and suppress them. Carole was not allowed to show her family when she was scared, sad or angry. 'Gordon often asked me why I looked so sad all the time. I didn't identify it as sadness then, but looking back that's what it was. I really wanted to belong somewhere else and not be part of that family. I had to pretend in front of other people that nothing was wrong.'

The effects are devastating. 'When these vital needs are frustrated and children are instead abused for the sake of the adults' needs by being exploited, beaten, punished, taken advantage of, manipulated, neglected, or deceived without the intervention of any witness, then their integrity will be lastingly impaired. The normal reactions to such injury should be anger and pain. Since children in this hurtful kind of environment, however, are forbidden to express their anger and since it would be unbearable to experience their pain alone, they are compelled to suppress their feelings, repress all memory of the trauma, and idealise all those guilty of the abuse. Later they will have no memory of what was done to them.'*

When the child's natural fascination with the world around leads her to point to her father's penis, or her mother's vagina or breasts, she is told what they are and given, verbally and non-verbally, messages about what is OK and not-OK. She is taught the rules and the parents do not define her behaviour as a sexual invitation.

Carole's father didn't allow her natural curiosity about sexuality to develop. She says 'I didn't like knowing the things I knew at such an early age. I didn't feel like a child, I didn't like knowing about babies at 7 or 8 years. He told me what intercourse was and that it was going to happen to me when I was old enough.'

Carole now knew things beyond the developmental stage she was at. At six and seven years of age children only think of their vaginas and genitals in terms of 'wee-wee' hole or 'front bottom'. She has no conception of what they could be used for, but once she is given the know-

* Alice Miller *Pictures of Childhood* Farrar, Strauss, New York, 1986.

ledge she can never go back to not knowing. She now has adult facts she has to keep secret, along with feelings of dismay at having this understanding.

In the 'good enough' family there are no secrets. Problems are resolved when they arise. Feelings are expressed. There are clear boundaries; both psychological and physical, every family member has their own identity. Relationships with people outside the family are encouraged.

If the child grows up in the 'good-enough' family where life feels predictable and her needs are met, even on a basic level, then she will develop physically and create an inner sense of security and trust which will form an adequate foundation for later life.

The child from the 'good enough' family grows up to form relationships, to enjoy herself, to be sure of herself, to have fun, to look after herself in a 'good enough' way. She expects people to be trustworthy.

If she learned trust and freedom then it will be relatively easy for her, as an adult, to form meaningful relationships with other people. She will believe she is OK. She will enter into adulthood with optimism, self-control, a feeling of adequacy and an integrated image of herself, and she will be open to a sense of fulfilment.

Our progress through our childhood can be likened to a pile of pennies. If we are a child in the 'good-enough' family our pile is straight and true. If we are a child in the abusive family, harm occurring during this time has the effect of a bent coin. The pile can no longer stand straight and each penny after the bent coin is affected. Just as the bent penny affects the ones coming after it so does childhood abuse affect adulthood.*

* Eric Berne

STROKING OR 'I KNOW YOU ARE THERE'

> I felt so pushed out when my brother was born and all the attention was on him, especially with three girls. I wanted desperately to be loved and noticed. It was the only time my father bothered about me. I hated it really but felt I had to be there and do as I was told. I felt special to someone.'

> I did steal once. I was desperate to gain attention *Sue*

When someone says how lovely you look or how good a certain piece of work was, when someone smiles warmly at you or when they hug you, you are being stroked. Stroking is about other people recognising us and our self-worth Our experience of stroking and the patterns people encounter go right back to early days of childhood. The important thing here is that 'it is a key that unlocks understanding of our patterns of behaviour and the legacy of our childhood that we choose to carry'.* It is another way we can understand and ultimately overcome our past.

We know that children need to be touched and recognised by their closest family. Stroking can be physical touch, a look, spoken – anything that tells the child she exists. Without stroking the child would find it difficult to grow up in an emotionally healthy way. Parents and other important figures often deny the child strokes or use them to train the child into certain roles and behaviours. Thus the abusive parent gives strokes in exchange for sexual touch or compliance from the child.

The child who doesn't receive enough positive attention seeks out any kind of attention, even if it is negative. Some children seek out their abusing parent, not because they want to be abused, but because they NEED the attention. Usually they are not getting these needs met

* Julie Hewson and Colin Turner 'Transactional Analysis in Management' (1991) The Staff College.

anywhere else and put up with the sexual side in order to get other needs met.* The basic rule is: any attention is better than none. Most of us would rather have some kind of attention than be totally ignored as if we didn't exist. If there are no positive then at least negative strokes reassure the child that she exists.

Stroking can also be negative – parents saying 'You're stupid' or 'You look a mess today'. It can also be physical – hitting, etc. It can be conditional, with strings attached: 'I'll give you this as long as you do something for me'. Or unconditional: 'I love you for who you are' or 'here's a present for you'. If she doesn't get enough stroking, then she will probably suffer emotionally later in life. If she gets enough, a in the 'good-enough' family she will develop into a healthy person who feels OK.

Stroking is the basis from which the child decides whether she is OK or not, whether others are OK, etc. Once this life position has been taken up it then guides everything she does. What happens is that when she does receive a stroke she will more than likely reject it in order to support the position she decided upon in childhood.

One of the fundamental tasks for the child to carry out is to seek out strokes from others. If she is stroked she will conclude that it is OK for her to be here – that she is OK. If she isn't, then she has to work out 'what must I do to get strokes'? The child is also more likely to repeat a behaviour if it gets her strokes. Stroking reinforces the behaviour which is stroked. So one person may please others in order to receive the strokes she desperately needs, anothermay by provoke people to get a reaction (any stroke is better than none), and so on. We can now understand why some of us repeat painful patterns time and time again, even though they *are* painful.

Carole got her recognition by not causing a fuss, pleasing others, DOING things (rather than BEING), denying herself, and so on. She was also ignored by her father when he wasn't abusing her. She says: 'I was never, ever cuddled by my parents. The only time I had a kiss was when I bought my mum some flowers on mother's day.

I was 7 or eight years old. If there was any praise it was for things done, never for myself.' Strokes were the way she learned about her value to others and therefore to herself.

She also says: 'I was never praised for any achievements, but was made to feel useless if I failed anything. So much was expected of me, but I wasn't allowed to expect anything back other than what I was used to – ignorance and abuse.' Carole's family stroked her negatively. She only got noticed for not doing things well enough. She says: 'I failed my exam because I am poor at maths and my father was furious with me and gave me a very hard time. He even went to school to make a fuss, he told the staff that I could be kept in at break times to do extra work. Nothing I ever did was good enough for him. I did quite well at shorthand but there was never any praise or encouragement.'

Carole was taught to live according to the expectations of others and learned that she could only get stroked negatively, if at all. She came to expect it and as an adult she sought strokes in the way she had been taught to do so as a child. This is not unusual, since we all feel safe with what we know best, whether good or bad. It is inevitable that in adulthood we will reproduce those patterns. Carole says: 'I was never satisfied with anything I did, at school, at work, or at home. Even now I need approval, even with the clothes I wear. If someone else didn't like a new item of clothing I would think twice about wearing it. Me liking it wouldn't be enough.'

She also set herself up to receive the negative strokes in relationships: 'Even when I had a relationship with a man who treated me very badly I put up with him because he always wanted me sexually. I found it difficult to let go. It was important to feel wanted, despite being treated so badly.'

Negative strokes carry more weight and significance than positive strokes and if these strokes are given by someone close, like a parent or someone you trust, then they will be even more powerful than from a distant relative. We know that Carole had some good influence in her life and was stroked by some relatives, but this was far outweighed by the negative stroking from her own parents. She says 'I was always surprised when any members of my extended family made a fuss of me'.

Donna also didn't receive strokes from her mother. She says: 'My mum never hugged me. I can never remember her arms protecting me or nurturing me in any way. I was pushed aside and it is hard to explain because I could never remember her being there, but when I went home at thirty years old I was really close to her, but she still never, even when my dad died, put her arm around me. She said You've got to get on with it and walked away.'

Because Donna didn't receive many or any strokes from her mother she took what she could from others even though this took the form of sexual contact with her brothers. She says: 'My older brother said I was special and there was no way I was going to jeopardise that, no way because I only had them to say I was special. I didn't get it from my mum.'

She received conditional strokes and this was later borne out in her adult life. She says: 'If someone was genuinely nice to me I would faint. At the back of my mind would always be 'what do you want?', because they would have to want something. Nobody could be nice without wanting something.'

If a child receives a lot of positive strokes in her growing years then she will grow up respecting and valuing herself and, importantly, assuming and believing others will respect and value her.

The child may stroke herself, believing others to be not-OK. She may find some comfort in being by herself away from the abuses of her family. Some children decide there are no positive strokes available and that they will have to rely on negative strokes to get by. The can last the rest of a child's life, so that even when a positive stroke is given to her she will reframe it as a negative stroke.

Depending on your life position ('I'm OK' etc) and your early experience of stroking you will develop a particular style of giving and receiving strokes. Women who have been abused tend to seek out negative strokes to maintain their deep-felt position of 'I'm not-OK'. One author writes 'The scared child receives an unnatural and unnecessary number of strokes, but eventually learns to expect them and to believe they are vital.'* The child from the 'good-enough' family will seek out positive strokes. It is very difficult to change this basic pattern, because there is a compulsion to repeat the same patterns which happened in childhood – but it can be done.

We create a stroke filter† which lets in some strokes but not others. We generally filter out those strokes which contradict the decisions we made in childhood, to maintain our view of ourselves and the world. Some strokes may be changed to let them through. When we said anything positive to Carole we would see a mismatch between what we were saying and her acceptance of it i.e. a sideways look and then downward glance. We could see she wasn't accepting it and might inwardly discount it or outwardly say 'It was nothing' and so on. When told her hair looked nice she would say 'Really, I think it is so out of condition', and so on.

This also meant that Carole could not stroke herself. When asked to write down good things about herself or ways to nurture herself, it proved very difficult for her.

She didn't allow herself to accept positive strokes because they didn't fit with her experience as a child and the way she felt about herself. She says: 'I have never thought of myself as being attractive physically. I am often surprised when something looks nice or fits me when I think it will be too small. I was surprised when a man said recently that I had nice legs. I think I look alright because I am clean and tidy but I don't see it as being attractive. I find that hard to believe.' What is so sad about his is that Carole is very beautiful, both in looks and personality, but it will take time to rid herself of her parents' programming.

* Claude Steiner *Script people Live*, Grove Press, Inc., 1974.
† Claude Steiner 'The Stroke Economy' TAJ 1, No. 3 July 1971 9–15.

Some women filter out all strokes, especially if their childhood has been painful and abusive. It feels too dangerous to let anything in, so they protect themselves but at the same time they deny themselves the positive strokes.

One therapist* talks of the five basic rules many parents instil in their offspring:

Don't give strokes if you have them to give
Don't ask for strokes when you need or want them
Don't accept strokes even if you want them
Don't reject strokes when you do not want them, or even if you do not like them
Don't give yourself strokes

This forms the foundation of the stroke economy† and is a good way of manipulating children. The child, in order to receive strokes, has to comply with her parents' wishes. Through therapy Carole learned and practised breaking the rules of the stroke economy. She began to ask for strokes, accept them and give herself them. The experience of her childhood was now no longer the case.

LIFE PLANS

'In the early states of embryonic development a slight wound, the mere prick of a pin, can not only cause severe alterations in, but may completely prevent, the development of whole limbs of the body. Just as if you have only one candle in a room and put your hand near the candle, half the room may become darkened, so if near the beginning of life you do only a little harm to the child, it may cast a shadow over the whole of its life'‡

*Claude Steiner
† Claude Steiner 'The Stroke Economy' TAJ 1: 3 July 1971
‡ Ferenzi – 1933.

I had a strong feeling that I was a horrible person. I blamed myself for EVERYTHING. I was unlovable, untrustworthy and useless. *Carole*

Everything you do as an adult you have done before as a child, but you didn't notice it' *Donna*

Even before the child can begin to speak she embarks on 'writing' her story – her life plan –[*] and as with other stories, she decides[†] on a beginning, middle and end.[‡] We develop ideas about who we are. We decide how we will live our life, who we will meet, how things will be and how our life will end.

In all our lives the dramatic events, and the roles we adopt and act out, are determined by our script and 'decided' on in childhood.

Our life plan makes our life follow a predictable pattern and it is the blueprint for a life course.[§]

Understanding our life plans or Script is an important building block to healing. Once we know what story we have written for ourselves then we can begin to find ways of changing it – if we want to.

We all had to create a life plan by the necessity to survive and have our needs met. We had to know how to get by in a world full of powerful grown-ups. There are three important factors when we form our life plan which have already been discussed in 'The world of the child'. The child is powerless and relies on her parents, she has immature thinking and inadequate ways of coping. These all go hand in hand with the formation of her life plan.

The basis of her life plan is written from birth to the age of about eight, with minor alterations in teenage years.

[*] S Woolams 'Formations of the Script' TAJ 3 No 1 Jan 1973 31–36.

[†] Decision – not meant in normal sense of the word but a conclusions possibly out of awareness which influence our future.

[‡] Known as Scripts – Claude Steiner.

[§] Claude Steiner *Scripts People Live* page 50.

She then has fixed ideas about who she is, who others are and the world around her. Some children may follow life plans which are tragic, like a soap opera, a comedy and so on.

The child born into an 'abusive' family, where the parents' needs are placed above her's, will begin by having her needs ignored. Even at this stage will begin to make judgements about herself, others and the world. She may decide 'I'm not-OK and it is not-OK for me to be here'. This directs everything she does. The child who believes herself to be not-OK will live out her life in a way which confirms that position.

We believe that all babies start off in life with an 'I'm OK, You're OK' position until something happens to cause them to assume another position. The child forms her life plan in response to this fundamental view of herself and others.

Therefore, the babies whose cries are repeatedly ignored will decide she probably shouldn't be here, that she is not-OK and that her feelings are not-OK either. If a young child's parents never respond predictably to her feelings of fear, sadness and frustration she soon learns it is unsafe to cry. She may even be told 'I'll give you something to cry about,' so she shuts off her feelings, because they cause too much trouble. Her immature mind deduces that if her feelings are not-OK she must not be OK, either'.

Our task in childhood is to lay down the foundations for our future through the various stages of development. The decisions we make in response to our experiences form the basis of how we think and behave in adult life.

We make decisions in an attempt to make sense of our world and these decisions create a permanent record, influencing everything we do. The earlier the decision is made, the greater its influence.

Once we have our expectations about ourselves, others and the world we tend to adapt and adjust new situations and experiences to support and strengthen our decisions. It feels safe to do this and every child is looking for and craving consistency and safety, even if this is essentially negative. Later in adulthood we continue to filter, concentrating on negatives and ignoring positives which do not 'fit' our life plan. A woman may believe 'I am a failure' rather than 'Some of the things I do go well, others don't go so well'.

The child, and consequently the adult, become hooked into a role based on her perception of 'what do I need to do to survive?'.

Children in the 'good enough' family have a better chance of deciding on a positive life plan. Abused children also make decisions – the most important decisions of their lives. It is therefore important to look at the processes which occurred in childhood and are now out of awareness but still being lived out today in adulthood.

We know that 45% of children who are abused are first abused under the age of 6 and 86% by the time they are ten.* We also know that the life plan is being formed at this time. From knowledge of child development we know these are crucial ages for the childs testing of 'Who am I?' and her experimentation with her personal power, social relationships and the consequences of her behaviour (i.e. 'If I do this then .. will happen). She also is establishing what it means to be the sex she is.

Many abused children fear they will not live to see another day, which is crucial to their early decisions. In abusive families the child's beliefs and awareness will inevitably be flawed, especially as she tries to make sense of what happens to her. As an adult, in order to heal she must acknowledge her childhood decisions.

A woman will not remember deciding on her life plan – it is now out of her awareness – but she is still living it out. It continues to affect and influence her relationships, her view of herself.

Since Carole's parents and family were the first people to show her how life was to be, and who she was, she had little chance of growing up with healthy perceptions and

* *Beyond Sexual Abuse*, D Jehu J Wiley and Sons 1989

beliefs about herself, others and the world around her.

Before she was born her family had built-in established rules which would curb her natural expression of thoughts, feelings and behaviour. At the least, she would have had to forsake her own needs for those of her family, but she had to endure more by having all her boundaries – her body, integrity and sexuality – ruthlessly assaulted.

Carole started 'writing' her life plan based on decisions which were a compromise between her own needs and survival with her parents and in her particular family. She decided early that she was 'worthless', unimportant, that others were more important and that reality took place on the outside. Carole says: 'My early experiences and beliefs were that I was unlovable, unimportant, worthless – just there to be used and abused. I felt overpowered and controlled, but at the same time abandoned, unprotected and sacrificed for the sake of peace in the everyday lives of the rest of my family.'

Carole's mother said nothing, even though she herself was physically abused by her husband – Carole talks about her mother being thrown out into the snow barefoot when she was seven months pregnant. She, by implication, caused Carole to think that in some way this must be normal and that she (Carole) was not OK for having the feelings she had. Such was the power of her beliefs that years later when Carole was at deaths door in hospital and her parents were called her father would not allow her mother to go to her daughter – and Carole accepted this.

The child feels a strong compulsion to believe in her parents and she may have decided that this is how things are.

Carole could not turn to her family or other adults for comfort because there would be a need to acknowledge that the abuse was happening. She had to adopt an image that all was well; her feelings were suppressed to protect the family.

Since her feelings were not cared for in her family as a child, she learned not to take care of them herself as an adult.

The abused child rarely experiences her feelings clearly in order to promote a healthy, positive identity. Her normal and expected reactions to experiences of abuse would be fear, anger, rage and anxiety, but since all feelings are unacceptable in the 'abusive' family she has to suppress them.

If she is not allowed to show her feelings and sees her feelings discounted she will learn to distrust them and make the major decision that her feelings are not-OK and that she is not-OK for having them.

If her parents ignore her thoughts and feelings and do not recognise her or 'stroke' her she decides it is not OK for her to exist and later in life she may kill herself. Alternatively, she may decide it is OK to exist provided she does what others want her to do and she pleases them.

Carole was also 'taught' by her family that she was only good for what she could do for others, not for who she was. She says: 'I was never cuddled by my parents. The only time I even had a kiss was when I bought my mother some flowers on Mothers Day – I was about seven or eight. If there was any praise it was always for things done, never for myself. Mum said one day when I was about nine that I shouldn't grumble when I was asked to help her; I always had to look after my sister Lana; Mum said she had grumbled the same to her mother and when her mother had died she was sorry.'

Through the abuse her father was teaching her she was only good for one thing.

When a child feels she is unlovable and worthless, like Carole, she tries to please and look after others in the hope that she can make herself lovable, worthy and important.

Carole found she continually did things to please others, never herself. She had difficulty saying 'no' and felt compelled to do what others wanted. She says: 'I was never allowed to make my own decisions – I always had to ask for permission. I was too frightened to be angry or to cry. I almost expected to be treated badly for some reason – there was a kind of safety in it.'

Carole did not realise that as an adult she did not have to do these things, but could be loved simply for being herself.

The life plan is based on childhood decisions and parental programming, and the child is given, overtly or covertly, *Don't* messages (known as injunctions). The common themes are *Don't Feel*; *Don't Be*; *Don't be you*; *Don't grow up*; *Don't be a child*; *Don't be close*; *Don't belong*; *Don't be sane* (or well) and *Don't think*. We are taught to cast off and disown parts of our natural abilities – our thinking, our feeling and so on.

Carole was not allowed to show her feelings and was given a very strong *Don't Feel* injunction by both her parents. She says: 'I remember withdrawing as a child – my feelings were totally ignored. I hardly ever cried.' All her life she received messages (overt and covert) that her feelings were unimportant. One moving episode came when, during her summer holidays, she followed her mother to work in tears, because she did not want to be left alone with her father. Her mother, although not knowing why Carole was behaving in this way, told her to go home, ignoring her feelings and even bent down to pick up some gravel from the driveway and throw it at her.

In the 'good enough' family, if something bad happens – for example, the death of a pet – the natural response is for the child to cry and to be comforted. If she is ignored and told to be quiet she will think it is wrong to show her feelings and maybe that there is something wrong with her for feeling the way she does.

In the 'good-enough' family parents help the child link her feelings with certain words. When she cries and looks sad her parents say 'Come here and give me a cuddle, why are you sad?'. The child learns that what she is feeling is sadness. She then learns to label her feelings and becomes able to say 'I'm sad' in order to have her needs met, i.e. by a cuddle and soothing words. The child decides her feelings are OK.

We are also given Permissions ('It's OK to . . . .') and, on the basis of the injunctions (*Don'ts*) and permissions, we make decisions about what to do and what not to do.

These messages are rarely given directly and are interpreted in the light of the child's current abilities (discussed in The World of the Child).

Donna was made to think everything was her fault: 'If anything went wrong it had to be my fault. Though I only got one spanking in my life from my father, my mother never touched me, but she used to cusp my brother across the side of the head, look at me and say why did you let him do that?. I might not even have been there'. The theme of everything being Donna's fault ran throughout her life.

Parents also give children rules for behaviour. For example 'Be good, be successful, keep things in the family'. These messages tend to be spoken and the child again makes decisions based on them.

The child may also 'swallow whole' things their parents say. For example, Berne relates the story of two men whose mother gave them overt messages of 'You'll end up in an asylum one day'. One became a psychiatrist and the other an in-patient. She may also 'swallow whole' beliefs, aspirations, views or opinions without dissecting them and incorporating what she wants to accept and ignoring what she wants to reject, thus making a healthy connection between what happens outside and inside her experience.

In the abusive family the child becomes confused and often can not know who she really is. Her world becomes one of conflicting messages; and because the family has no open communication she is left not knowing what is happening. As in Donna's experience she has done nothing wrong and knows it inside, but from the outside she is blamed for someone else's behaviour.

Like many children, Carole accepted definitions of herself supplied by abusive others – not ones based on reality or on who she felt she was. Thus as an adult she found it extremely difficult to allow her adult awareness to override her belief that she was worthless and unlovable. She wouldn't allow good and positive messages to pass through her filter.

During the time of life-plan formation the child may take negative statements and turn them into positive ones. For example, 'little girls shouldn't be angry' can become 'but it is OK for adult women to be angry'.

Parents may also model to children 'here's how to . . .' messages. For example, to cook, write, hide your feelings, to be unhappy. Carole, through her mothers modelling, learned to ignore her feelings and become depressed.

Messages about who you were were continually given. If your parents told you you were pretty, clever and thoughtful then you would probably develop a positive image of yourself. If they told you you were bad, stupid and wicked then your self-esteem would be low and you would develop a negative image of yourself. You might have been given messages in the form of 'You are just like your aunty Sarah' and aunty Sarah just happens to have been a loud-mouthed, drunkard whom no-one respected. Or you may have been told 'She's not at all like her sister', who was seen as good, bright.

These messages may not be accurate, but as a child you would still have believed in them and made your decisions on the basis of them. Because of this they still affect you today. As a child you accepted (because you had to) a false image of yourself.

Negative messages can only hinder healing.

As adults we may be able to hear some messages in our heads and link them back to a specific person. As Donna says: 'The only thing my mother ever taught me to do was cook. She said I was too stupid to do anything else, so I would have to be a wife with kids. The family, especially my mother, used to tell me I was stupid and at school it was easier for me to be stupid because the harder I tried the worse it became, so I just sat there and was dumb. When I decided to speak out about the abuse I said to my sister-in-law 'Please don't say I'm stupid'. I was petrified that she would. She didn't but it was at the back of my mind. Sometimes it is still there – some people say you're stupid and it sinks in. There is a little voice which warns me off from opening my mouth even now'. No-one who meets Donna would ever feel she is stupid – she is bright and has a lot to say.

Another woman talked of hearing her mother's voice saying 'you're dirty and bad' whenever she expressed her feelings.

there are other messages which we can not put actual words to but can feel and show in our behaviour. For example *Don't be* and *Don't Exist* could show up as us having accidents, not eating, excessive smoking and drinking.

The child can always take on board messages whole, interpret them or ignore them, or use one message to guard against another: 'I can exist as long as I don't feel my feelings'.

Women may ask themselves why they always meet the same kind of man or end up in the same situation time and time again. As Donna says: 'After you've been abused you tend to fall into abusive relationships with men, and women – they find you. I used to have a standing joke with a friend that when I went out fluorescent lights flashed on my head saying 'This one is easy' – it is just something you put across. You always attract the same people. I don't think I've had anyone who hasn't used me in some way for something. This will be the hardest pattern to break. If I met someone who was genuinely nice to me I think I would faint. At the back of my mind would always be the question – what does he want? To me they would always want something.'

Knowing and understanding your life plan will help you appreciate why you fall into certain patterns, especially painful ones.

It is important to remember that our life plan is based on a child's interpretation of what happens to her and the way she feels. She is highly vulnerable, both physically and intellectually, and perceives the world completely differently from adults. She makes decisions because she has to as a matter of life or death. The younger the child is when she makes her life plan decisions, the more dysfunctional these decisions are likely to be in her adult life, but she is compelled to follow her life plan.

Life plans are limiting. They set restrictions on development and govern important aspects of your life – we will often choose people to be our friends and lovers because they complement our life plan. In her adult life Carole consistently 'chose' men who ignored her feelings because it fitted with her life plan. Your life plan will affect what kind of job you will have, whether you will be a success or failure, your expectations and so on.

When we are using our life plan we tend to meet problems in our adult life by re-playing childhood strategies, which in turn reinforces our view of ourselves, others and the world.

Life plan decisions are made usually over a period of time, but isolated incidents such as abuse can cause the child to make a central life plan decision. For example 'I will never get close to a man again'. Or in Donna's experience 'If I was going to show someone I loved them, it would be through sex. It was the only way I was taught'.

Parents give messages week in, and week out, and some are good and some bad. They can not make the decision for the child but can exert a major influence on her life plan decisions and, consequently, her feelings, thinking and behaviour. Donna says: 'Everyone kept telling me I was stupid so I became a loner – it was my way of coping. I just went off and did my own thing, and when I was by myself nobody could say 'don't do that, it is wrong', 'don't do that it is stupid' or 'don't be so dumb'.

The younger she is the more susceptible the child is, so the more her developmental skills and life experiences are contaminated. She has fewer resources to draw on in the face of a trauma. The abuser is giving her powerful messages about the kind of world she dwells in and who she is. She will make decisions based on these messages.

If the abuse occurs over several developmental stages there will be spaces and gaps as the child grows older. Across time in the 'good enough' family she will make 'OK' decisions about being, doing, thinking, her identity, separation, sexual development.

The child from the 'abusive' family will, because of the

abuse and lack of consistency of care, nurturing and safety, make poor decisions about herself other people and life itself. She may have a strong drive to harm herself which is not necessarily conscious but is the result of her decisions not to be and not to exist.

For example, Carole knew she had this drive and kept little petrol in her car to avoid killing herself by carbon-monoxide poisoning. Other aspects of her behaviour included not protecting herself by walking alone at night, for example.

The child from the abusive family may also create a life plan which causes her continually to fail, be depressed, attempt suicide or end with suicide, death or in an institution.

Her present is based on traumatic, unhappy past conclusions. She represses her needs in order to protect herself. For example, a life plan decision not to be close to others was, at one time, needed for survival. As Carole says: 'I remember being in the playground once on a very hot day and a boy was talking to me. He was about 12, he wanted to hold my hand, and I remember thinking I didn't want to do that; he was very nice and I didn't know why I didn't want to, and that made me feel different and strange. Most children want to be like everyone else don't they?'

Because of the unpleasant touch the child will make decisions that people are not to be trusted, that she is worthless, that life is frightening and so on. She will 'expect' bad things to happen because that is what she decided and has had reinforced by others. She sees the world from the position of 'I'm not-OK, others are' 'I'm not-OK, others are not-OK too'. The negative messages she receives distort her view of herself and her growth.

She may decide to separate emotionally from her body – denying the reality of what she is feeling. Carole made some important early decisions that her feelings didn't matter and were unacceptable. After years of being unable to trust others and having her feelings ignored she minimised and suppressed them.

When Carole's father physically abused her mother

and verbally abused her grandmother she noticed that her mother or grandmother did nothing, so she decided they were all there to keep her father happy and her needs were not important.

Feelings were not-OK in Carole's family. So she learned to ignore them and became depressed. She also made decisions to cut off from her body. She says: 'I do not think about my body,' disowning the first signs of feelings, so how could she even know how she felt?

If her parents had taken notice of her feelings, modelled healthy emotions, given her time, comforted her when she was upset and made things better for her she could have decided her feelings were OK and it was OK to experience and express them. She would have been able to give her inside feelings an outside label (I am sad, angry and so on) and create a set of behaviours. For example, she would know if she was upset because she could cry and approach her parents for comfort; and the feeling would then go away.

The continual warping of Carole's reality through the family's denial caused her to feel crazy. As a child she had a choice – believe what her parents said and did, or believe herself and her feelings. She doubted her own feelings and lost her sense of her self. Her reality and experience were ignored. If everyone around you pretends nothing has happened, you doubt yourself.

All Carole's childhood was spent trying to figure out how to get by and be good, but what she was trying to make sense of was beyond explanation, certainly that of a child. It was a bewildering time for her and all she had to work on were her parents' actions and words, so she learned that she could not depend on her feelings because they did not help her survive. Feelings got her into more trouble. She could not know what reality was, because her feelings did not match actual events. For example, the abuse caused her intense pain and scare (internal experience) but outside her nobody was reacting to this; they disregarded her. It is no wonder she felt crazy.

The best way she could survive in her family was not to feel, not to tell and not to trust, and she entered adulthood under the influence of these childhood decisions.

Carole, as an adult, believed others would not be there for her – emotionally or physically – because she had not experienced this as a child. To trust, you need to feel safe and encounter consistency from others. If the child's feelings are respected and validated she can develop a sense of self worth. It is not enough for the child to hear she is loved, she needs to have it shown to her. Only then can she believe it.

Other victims saw and heard mixed messages which led them to mistrust others. Parents may tell the child what she is feeling and reassure the child all is OK when her experience tells her it is not.

The child soon decides others can not be trusted and her feelings can not be trusted.

The victim of abuse may have her thinking overlooked, ignored or put down. She then has an important source of information about herself taken away and discounted. She becomes confused and the systematic attack on her thinking and feeling leave her unable to recognise what she understand the world to be and what she is told about the world. Secrets and lies cause her to become mindless. She fears she is going crazy because reality does not fit in with her experiences and feelings. Craziness, or a feeling of craziness, is the result of a childhood series of lies, discounts and a lack of positive nurturing and support.

The victim of abuse becomes 'split'. A whole part of her is not acknowledged and is cut off, often not even felt. The feelings continue to exist, though gradually building up and affecting her body state, and her behaviour. Eventually they find a way of expressing themselves through illness and other forms.

The child from the 'good enough' family might not remember or have little memory of positive touch but will decide people can be trusted. Because she has decided people are essentially trustworthy she will expect trust and, therefore, create it.

After abuse the child's world will never be the same again. Her view of herself, others and the world has to be changed to fit in with this powerful new experience. The experience of sexual abuse destroys her capacity for spontaneity, intimacy and joy in life.

Abuse distorts and limits her capacity in adulthood.

Our life plan is meant to last a lifetime and we reinforce it continually. Once we have developed our expectations about ourselves, others and the world around we will adapt to new situations to support and reinforce our early decisions. We will say to ourselves 'See, I was right to make that decision/choice, as it was the only one possible'.

Donna says: 'When you do trust, you put your trust in the wrong people. You follow the pattern all the time and each time your trust is broken. As a child, as an innocent, you put your trust in adults and they betray you. As you go on in life you continue the pattern, so eventually you don't trust anybody.'

It feels safe to follow our life plan as an adult, and as a child each of us is looking for consistency and safety, even if it is negative. Carole says 'One day I got on the wrong bus after school. I was very scared about being on the wrong bus. I didn't want to be at home, but I also did not want to be there. Either way it spelt trouble.'

The child who does not receive the loving she needs will accept punishment or negative strokes as a substitute – anything is better than being ignored.

One theorist says 'The original decisions was made out of a need to survive in the face of destructive parental behaviours, and until that threat of punishment is changed, the decisions must be maintained'.*

The threat is still there in adulthood and may show itself in many ways. For example, when Carole talked about her family's secrets during therapy she was acting against strong and potent messages of 'Don't talk, Don't

* Erskine page 191.

trust, and *Don't feel*'.* She was also breaking the message of 'Don't be important'. Each time she would raise her hand to her mouth or throat, indicating to us that her father's threats to keep the secret at all costs were still potent, even at the age of 51. Her body signals were showing her life plan decisions. Other indications came when Carole cleared her throat, talked quietly and found herself not being able to write her experiences down. Later she discovered two cysts either side of her throat.

A lot of experiences, negative and positive, are sifted so they fit our life plans.

Changing our life plan is hard, but Donna has started the process: 'I passed a test in work last week and I was the only one who passed. In all my life I have never passed anything and if someone said there's a test I'd fall apart. I have done my job for five years and if I had to do a test I could guarantee I wouldn't be able to do it. At the back of my mind is 'You're stupid – you can't do it'. When I got the results of the test and a certificate saying I'd passed I was over the moon. I know it is trivial but to me it is the biggest thing I have ever done. I had finally achieved something. I have broken the pattern, because that is the step to changing. I've broken the pattern of being stupid.'

She also says: 'When I went out with my boyfriend, he beat me and went off with other women. Even now he will tell me I'm a whore and dog. And I take it because I was brought up like that – I didn't know any different. It is so natural to stand there and take it. It wasn't until recently I stood up to him and said 'don't you dare, you have no right to call me that'. Two years ago I would never have done that. I would have taken it, cowered and thought maybe I *am* a whore.'

Even as an adult we perceive any threat to our life plan-based view of the world as a threat to the satisfaction of

* Claudia Black *It will never happen to me*, MAC Publishers, Denver 1981, page 3. Three rules of aloholic families which can be applied to the 'abusive' family.

our needs and even to our survival. Carole had to stick to her life plan because she feared what would happen if she broke the rules. To show her true feelings meant breaking the secrecy of her family and her childhood.

The penalty for telling and showing her true feelings was, at worst, death. She would feel more comfortable, like all of us, going with her life plan even though she could see she was damaging herself, because it was still less bad than the 'real' threat. When we defy our life plan we experience a great deal of tension in our bodies and perhaps feelings of scare.

What you have to remember is that the early decisions which continue to affect your life today were based on inadequate information. Conscious or unconscious childhood perceptions, accurate or flawed, influence the way we view ourselves, others and the world around us.

The World of the Adult

Damaged Goods

Perfection, all shiny and clean.
No longer good enough
for the best in the land
with a good reputation,
sent packing
to Tesco's with a label
Bargain – slight second
why will no-one buy?
Shop soiled – dirty
sent to the market
surely to sell here.
 No takers – too damaged
Don't merit a stall space
sent out
with the garbage
clear no-one will want me now
too ugly – too dirty
But I coulda been sold in Harrods
if you had just
Handled with care.

Anonymous Survivor

Carole

'I have always had a clear memory of what happened; it has never left me. I don't think I allowed Brian or anybody else to be really close to me – I think I was afraid to trust anybody. The only person I really felt safe with was Gordon, and I couldn't even confide in him until I was desperate. I think Brian wanted to pretend the abuse hadn't happened because he thought talking about it wouldn't necessarily help me. Even when I had a relationship with a man who treated me very badly I put up with him because he always wanted me – I found it very difficult to let go. It was important to feel wanted, despite being treated so badly.

When I was having a difficult time in my marriage, I overdosed on pills and alcohol. I was staying with a friend at the time, and she asked me what was wrong, so I told her what I had done. I was taken to hospital to have my stomach pumped out. I haven't made any other suicide attempts but the thought has crossed my mind many times. I remember going to a chemist to buy some tablets during my time with the therapy group but it was closed – that was enough to make me think again. Sometimes life doesn't seem worth the hassle, which seems strange because I didn't think that when the awful things were happening to me.'

EFFECTS

In a letter to her father, Sue says: 'The abuse has affected my life in so many ways. I wonder if you have been affected by it? I feel my childhood was taken away from me – all the growing-up years, the years which should have been carefree. I never learned to love properly, I rushed into a relationship and clung like ivy, not daring to let go because I was afraid of being on my own. I was desperately in love.. or so I thought. I wanted to leave home to get away from you. Marriage was the answer.'

'My whole life has been affected.' *Donna*

'To be sexually exploited by a known and trusted adult is a central and formative experience in the lives of countless women.' 'The preponderance of evidence suggests that for any child sexual contact with an adult, especially a trusted relative, is a significant trauma which may have long-lasting deleterious effects. The sexual trauma does not necessarily lead to the development of a major mental illness.'[*]

'My behaviour had been a normal response to abnormal circumstances, circumstances so harshly oppressive that I had been unable to shed their presence within me, even as an adult.'[†]

The impact of abuse regardless of its type or duration can result in a woman having severe problems as an adult. As discovered earlier in this book, the immediate impact on the child results in feelings of isolation, shame, guilt, helplessness and hopelessness. The long term effects of abuse may lead to problems which are not seen to be connected to the past – feelings of isolation, depression,

[*] J L Herman (1981) *Father and Daughter Incest*, Harvard University Press.
[†] J Spring *Cry Hard and Swim*, Virago Press, 1987.

anxiety, guilt, shame, grief, deep feelings of worthlessness which can not be shaken off. There can also be
behaviour problems – eating disorders, disturbed sleep
patterns, mood swings, panic attacks, phobias, difficulty
in relating to others and sexual problems. The way we
think can be affected, also – believing we are not important, being suspicious, blocking out feelings and being
unable to stop thinking about the past.

The effects survivors list can seem endless, but it is
important to remember we all have problems. These effects are not just related to having experienced abuse, but
are a normal reaction to traumatic events. When we stud-
ied how the child's personality develops we saw that
each experience was built on, like a pile of pennies. The
abuse could cause the pile to lean off centre and, therefore, affect the way we viewed and responded to the
world. Of course, other childhood events can have a
similar effect – the loss of a parent or sibling, a life threatening illness, being moved from place to place and so on.

It is possible to overcome the effects of abuse. The adult
has been shaped by childhood experiences, resulting in
ways of thinking and behaving which are unrewarding
for her, but she can deal with these – the pile of pennies
can be brought back into line.

The effects of the abuse are influenced by many things –
the identity of the perpetrator, the degree of closeness,
authority, their power, the number of abusers – and each
woman's response will be unique as a result. It is often
difficult to separate the effects of the abuse from the effects
of growing up in an 'abusive' family which will have
reinforced the beliefs the child has developed during the
abuse, after the abuse has finished or if the abuse took
place outside the close family unit. It has been suggested
that the earlier the abuse takes place the greater the consequences when the child becomes the adult, and that where
the sexual abuse has been accompanied by physical force
or violence the effects are even more damaging.

Women are often aware that their lives are not as they
would like them. Perhaps they find themselves repeating

patterns in relationships, being unable to give up drinking or smoking, or maybe wanting to feel more confident
and set goals for themselves, but they are unable to make
the first move. Survivors may not make the connection
between the things which are causing them difficulty
now and the experiences of their past. For many years in
adulthood, Carole suffered from irritable bowel syndrome
whenever she was upset or felt threatened. She did not
understand that this was a legacy from her childhood, her
body's way of responding to the suppressed fear which
was triggered by any upset she experienced as an adult.

For some women life becomes so difficult that they feel
they need professional help to understand their situation
and make changes. Many go into therapy, or approach
hypnotherapists or alternative practitioners, to deal with
the symptoms rather than the cause. Many survivors
have a long history of contact with their GP without the
abuse ever being mentioned. Some can cope without
therapy, others not. It could be that the former have
simply 'resigned' themselves to the effects of the abuse.

Personality

The 'relationships between the growing individual and
the people in his life form the basic factor around which
personality develops.'[*]

As we have discovered for victims of abuse the daily
struggle to cope with and survive their experience, perpetrated by others, can have a major effect on how they
develop into adult personalities. The loss of love and
nurturing, loss of family and the easy-going atmosphere
of childhood, loss of self-confidence and self esteem, loss
of spontaneity and intimacy, loss of trust in the environment and the ability to distinguish dangerous people,
loss of the right to be 'normal' – these can all be concealed
by being successful, bright, funny and so on and therefore
no-one knows the secret loss of not being able to grow up

* *Hello Sigmund, this is Eric Sheed,* Andrews and McNeel, 1978

at a normal pace. You can not go back but you CAN recover from the effects of these losses.

You became the person you are today in order to survive – that survival is a celebration in itself. Some of the ways in which you survived as a child will stand you in good stead for the rest of your life, while others will be less useful to you as an adult. You can free yourself of those behaviour patterns which are no longer useful to you and which leave you feeling depressed or frustrated.

The effects of the losses are numerous and varied – for example, not feeling your feelings, a lack of awareness, depression, an inability to trust others, excessive vigilance, a need to over-achieve. Low self-esteem comes from the child perceiving herself to be to blame – the adult grows up to feel she is guilty, unworthy, dirty, bad and at fault. Even with the benefit of adult thinking she finds it difficult to see herself as ever being childlike, so she can not see how she was not responsible for the abuse.

Having a part of your life, and the thoughts and feelings associated with it, unconsciously suppressed or consciously hidden can lead to a feeling of not quite knowing who you really are and not quite feeling OK. When we experience ourselves as healthy individuals we feel integrated. We see ourselves as 'whole' and behave consistently – there is an essential personality. Most women survivors have a lack of acceptance and faith in who they are they are unsure whether they can trust themselves, what they know and what they feel. They find it difficult to have an integrated personality, to feel a sense of wholeness, but rather separate parts of themselves off and act differently with different people and in different situations. This is something we all do to some degree – it keeps us comfortable and safe – but for the survivor it may be exaggerated and detrimental to her happiness. She may find herself presenting a part of her personality which does not achieve what she wants. This echoes the experience of the abused child who had to live a life of pretence. Life was fragmented – her real self split from her false self. The lack of control she experienced over others, her body, and deciding what was right and wrong, leads her to lose her sense of self. As a child she had to do as she was told. She was not allowed to function as an individual. She had to follow the family rules. She was not allowed to 'be' who she really was.

Through her therapy Carole could discover and experience being known and seen as a whole person. She was free to show *herself*. No longer did she have to feel fragmented – she could discover and reclaim the 'real' Carole.

The survivor often feels like an imperfect person waiting to be found out. She believes the rest of the world is OK and thinks she must get everything right to be OK. However none of us can achieve perfection and so the survivor is left feeling 'I can never do anything well'.

Feeling bad about yourself, dirty, or hating your body, often leads to a self consciousness, a belief that people can somehow detect that you have been abused. Many women believe that because of what they have been through they are fit only to be used and abused by others. They have very low expectations of others, believing everyone will let them down.

Survivors often behave in ways which will test those round them, and when their expectations are fulfilled they use this to confirm how undeserving and awful they are. When a situation or a relationship does go well it is often accompanied by a belief that everything has to be 'paid for' in the end. Feelings of happiness bring with them a fear that at any moment something will happen to take those feelings away.

While for some women the struggle to survive their past may lead to a psychological breakdown, others may experience less severe problems. Some women may have compulsive behaviours. This can take the form of compulsive lying, which may have started with the need in childhood to lie to hide the abuse. Other compulsions include shopping for food to support an eating disorder, or perhaps for clothes or items which are not really required. This can take the form of filling the empty space within, rather like trying to fill up a bottomless bucket.

Some survivors develop an obsession with certain thoughts or behaviours. They may become excessively concerned with cleaning their home, or keeping their children spotless. Sue says: 'I felt I was overprotective with cleanliness and making the girls cover their private parts. I was always washing.'

Some women find themselves constantly fearing harm to those close to them, and becoming obsessed with knowing where and what those individuals are doing. In these cases the behaviour is an attempt to gain control over her life, so being prevented from carrying it out can lead to acute anxiety and fear. Obsessive behaviour may also help to prevent past experiences from surfacing in the form of memory or even flashbacks.

The lack of boundaries between the child and her abuser can lead to an inability to separate the self from others during familiar experiences in adulthood. For example, being able to know that the baby suckling you is not the abuser, nor is the partner making love with you. If we don't separate effectively these distortions can continue to affect our sexuality, our beliefs about our bodies, parenting and so on. Failure to separate the abuser from others in our lives prevents us from challenging our fear. We will continue to be fearful if we class all people as abusers or potential abusers.

Some women who have been abused show self-destructive tendencies. As a result of feeling bad about themselves and feeling unworthy of anyone else's concern, they may abuse their bodies through drink or drugs, or by putting themselves at risk. They continually hurt themselves in domestic accidents by being careless and unaware of dangers. Some survivors place themselves in positions where they experience physical pain as a way of cancelling the emotional pain they are unable to deal with. Some will hurt themselves physically, by cutting or burning themselves as a way of releasing the pain in a 'safe way'. They may also create situations so they are continually faced with an emotional crisis, thus preventing them from having to deal with the emotional crisis from the past. For those who love and care for the woman it can be difficult to understand and cope with some of this behaviour.

Self Esteem

'I didn't like myself at all – I was just a tart.' *Donna*

'I have tried to hurt myself in the past by taking too many sleeping pills, and I was always playing the love game by hurting men and playing around all the time. My main punishment, though, is self-worth – I don't believe even now that I am worth any praise or love.' *Tracy*

Abuse shatters self esteem and leaves the woman with an unreal picture of herself and a damaged, negative sense of self. She feels, helpless, hopeless, powerless, worthless and different, and these feelings may be compounded by her sense of guilt and shame about the abuse and her inability to stop it. Survivors are hard on themselves, blaming themselves for everything which goes wrong and feeling guilty for being unable to meet other peoples demands. The sense of powerlessness and its resulting lack of assertion, leaves her unable to protect herself from further exploitation or to ask for what she needs. She does not like herself and can not understand how others like her. She tells herself there is no way others can be right about her because they don't really know her. If they were to really know what she was like inside they would realise they were wrong. Therefore, what does their opinion amount to anyway?

She is aware of her inability to trust anyone, but because she believes it was her fault that her trust was broken in the first place she can use her mistrust as self punishment – i.e. 'I don't deserve to have someone I can really trust'. Her sense of self may be so low that her resulting self hatred is expressed as hostility toward other people, which in turn results in further alienation and isolation from them, proving to her how unlovable she is.

As a child the victim had little chance to check the

negative view of herself with reality. The abuse and abuser distorted her reality. This negative image was perpetuated by the tight boundaries of the abusive family in order to maintain secrecy.

Though many survivors deal with their problems with great strength and courage born out of their ability to cope and survive as children, they are unable to recognise these qualities in adulthood.

Body

'I felt fear and disgust about my body – sometimes, not all of the time.' *Donna*

'I do not like my body and do not get any pleasure from looking at it or touching it. I have a fear of sex and am not interested.' *Jackie*

'The body is the guardian both of the most deeply hidden or denied feelings and of those which are permitted and expressed.'*

The experience of abuse is physical and emotional. The child is in the process of developing her ideas about her body when she is abused, leading to distorted views. She may see her body as dirty, ugly, bad, out of control or untrustworthy. Some survivors will avoid looking after themselves, ignoring physical symptoms and not taking responsibility for any illnesses. During the writing of this book, Carole noticed a quite large and painful lump in her throat but had to be coerced into visiting her doctor. It was as if her body and health were not seen as being important.

Survivors often find it difficult to think of themselves as attractive and see themselves as ugly as a result of the abuse. They may find it difficult to accept positive comments about their personal appearance, and are highly sensitive to what they consider to be 'defects' in their physical appearance, associating them with inner flaws.

You may hate your body believing it has let you down.

* S. Ligabue "The somatic component of the script in early development" TAJ Vol 21, No 1, January 1991

This may be expressed by continuing to damage it through over-eating, drug abuse or self mutilation. Feeling disgusting and ugly inside may lead to 'beating yourself up' because you believe you deserve to be punished. You may feel anger, guilt and shame when you think about your body.

You may not hate your body but you feel detached from it as though it does not really belong to you. Abused children have been trained to think of themselves as bodies to be used for adults' ends. They are 'objects' and, therefore, discount feelings of discomfort and pain. Their experience of having no rights over it, of having their personal boundaries ignored, can lead them to feel that their body was possessed by the abuser. They may feel that they have no control over it, that they can not make it do what they want or predict how it will respond. This is particularly likely to happen if, as a child, they used disassociation during the incidents of abuse. The child may anaesthetise parts of her body, becoming physically numb or, in some cases, split totally from her body, letting her mind detach itself completely from what is happening to her body. This way of coping allows her to survive and make the experience 'bearable'.

In a few women, the feeling of disassociation manifests itself in feeling that they are not really female and in feeling a need to distance themselves from the vulnerability they associate with being female. Many women associate the female parts of their body with fear of abuse and avoid revealing the feminine aspects of themselves, dressing in loose, colourless clothing and avoiding situations where their body in on display – going to the gym, swimming and so on. Weight gain is often used to disguise their shape and make them less attractive and 'desirable'.

Donna says: 'I began to put on weight when I went back home. My brother said how lovely I looked and all the rest of that rubbish – big tits and so on. That was when I started using food and alcohol. I thought if I put on weight and changed my appearance I wouldn't look so good, and by not looking good they wouldn't want me. My weight gain was unconscious to start with. When I was pregnant and had my son I put on quite a bit of weight, then lost it all and went down from 11 stone to 8 stone. I stayed there for a number of years. Then I went home and everyone was so amazed I had lost all of my weight that somewhere in the back of my mind I said to myself 'put it back on quick', so I did. I just piled it all back on and then never stopped. If someone says to me now 'you look nice', or something, I will eat something. I don't do as much as I used to because I don't like the effect it has.'

When women begin to heal, the change can be seen in their appearance. As they begin to feel better about themselves they pay more attention to how they look and what they wear.

Health

'I think most women who are abused suffer from kidney infections, thrush and goodness knows what – anything to do with that part of the body.' *Donna*

Many survivors experience health problems mainly associated with stress-related disorders. Many of the symptoms of Post Traumatic Stress Syndrome – a range of psychological and physical effects which can occur after an individual has been traumatised through injury or being part of, or witnessing, a shocking event – continue for years, but may have started in childhood. These include panic attacks, sleeping disorders, general anxiety and a high level of flashback activity where the incidents are re-experienced physically and emotionally.

Women who have developed physical ailments – for example, digestive disorders or migraine headaches – as a result of repressing their feelings may continue to experience them long after the abuse has ended. This way of coping with the situation may also have had the added advantage of helping them avoid the abuse as children.

Though women who have been sexually abused may experience gynaecological problems as a result of physical damage, many of the illnesses experienced are of a somatic nature – psychological in origin but physical in their manifestation. They may have resulted from the body's need to 'shut down' in the face of a terrorfying situation. They are a safer way for woman to express the damage and pain they experienced and an indication of a need for healing.

Victims of abuse had the control over their bodies and their lives taken away from them when they were children, so their difficulty with control as adults may be reflected in their relationship with food. Eating disorders may take the form of compulsive eating, leading to obesity when the woman is unable to control her food intake. She may have started over-eating in childhood to comfort herself, or in an attempt to make herself unattractive. Her weight gain increases her poor self-image and low self-esteem.

Other women may use food to create a feeling of control by secret bingeing followed by self-induced vomiting, known as Bulimia Nervosa, continues to promote feelings of guilt and shame. Anorexia Nervosa – self starving and purging through laxatives as well as self-induced vomiting – is again an attempt to exercise control over body shape, size and maturity, and is experienced by many women who have survived abuse. At an eating disorders clinic, of 78 women 64 percent had been sexually abused, 80 percent children.*

Some women see illness as another betrayal – their body has let them down increasing their belief that they have little control. Being ill may also confirm their belief that they are damaged or internally abnormal as a result of the abuse. Others will be so split from their body that they will be unaware of the strain they put on their physical self and may be the last person to acknowledge that they are unwell. They put themselves at risk through excessive smoking, poor diet and so on, and avoid medical checks. They often have a much higher pain threshold than normal.

* Our Bodies Ourselves

These responses are the result of their physical needs not being met during childhood and the belief that their physical well being was of no importance. Carole was never taught to take care of her physical needs. When she had a hysterectomy and came out of hospital her husband had persuaded her to go out for the evening – she consequently haemorrhaged and had to go back to hospital to be cared for. She ignored her own needs, leading to physical danger. Given the childhood experience she describes, it is not surprising that she responded in this way.

'I was never taught how to look after myself. I was never given the proper underwear, especially when I was a teenager and needed a bra. I remember stealing one from my mother's drawer and wearing it until it was so dirty I couldn't wear it any longer. I felt ashamed to admit I needed it and my mother showed no signs of recognising that I needed one. She couldn't cope with my needs apart from the 'safe' things such as shoes, school uniform and so on. I was never given a deodorant to use – My Aunty Jane gave me my first one when she came to visit in Southsea. When I had my period I had to use pieces of old towel for protection because I was never given sanitary towels. I probably wore the same piece of towel for about three days which made me really sore and created a terrible smell. I didn't know what else to do – I thought that was how it had to be. I was so sore all the skin round my vagina peeled away.'

Women may also ignore physical symptoms to avoid contact with the medical profession. They may fear being touched by strangers or may experience flashbacks during an examination. Before Carole had ever disclosed her abuse to anyone other than her partners, she was asked during a gynaecological examination at what age she had first experienced sex. She was so shocked that she was unable to answer and the woman doctor tactfully said: 'I'll just put down early then'.

Carole says: 'But because I didn't want her to think I had been a promiscuous teenager I eventually managed to say 'yes, but not with my consent.' It was important to me to make that point clear. I am fortunate that I have never felt the abuse was my fault so guilt has never been a problem for me as it has been for many other survivors. For this reason I wanted this doctor to know I was not responsible for having sex early in my life even though I couldn't explain why.''

We can learn how to use our physical symptoms to find more out about ourselves. Each time Carole now has a stomach upset she will not automatically assume it is physical but look to her feelings first.

Relationships

'After you've been abused you fall into relationships with men and women which are not good – they find you. My husband was a womaniser – he never beat me up but sex was everything to him morning noon and night. He used to come home from work during the day for it. He was an abuser and because I was always the victim I stayed the victim – you always stay the victim. When I went out with another man he beat me. He went off with other women and even now will tell me how stupid I am and that I'm a whore and a dog. I take it because I've been brought up like that. I don't know any different – it is natural to stand there and take it. It wasn't until recently that I stood up to him and said 'don't you dare speak to me like that. You have no right to call me that', but two years ago, before my healing, I would never have done that. It was always my fault – everything was my fault so I took it.

I used to have standing joke with my mate when I went out with her about fluorescent lights flashing on my head saying this one is easy. It is something which I put across automatically. Men will use you for what they can get – you always attract the same kind of people. I don't think I have any friends or anybody who hasn't used me in some way for something. They always want something from me and they always take it. This will be the hardest pattern to break.' Donna

Any tension between the child and parent relationship

will inevitably affect the childs attempt to make meaningful relationships later in life. The patterns may be many
and are certainly not only the result of abuse – many
women who have not experienced abuse will recognise
them as part of their own lives.

The lack of trust generated from childhood and the
feelings of basic insecurity, because the childs needs were
never met, may lead the adult to test out their partners
and provoke rejection.

For many survivors their feelings of depression and
loneliness leave them with little hope of having a rewarding relationship, but at the same time they still seek the
caring and nurturing they missed in childhood. The strong
desire for love and attention are unmet child needs and
can not always be met through the adult.

Having been prevented from asserting or protecting
herself as a child, the adult survivor lacks the skills needed
in her relationships, which may lead her into further
abusive situations — physical and mental violence. Many
survivors have a history of damaging and abusive personal relationships.

One of the common ways we attempt to deal with
trauma and its effects is to re-create situations and events
which repeat the original. We do this to try and gain
control, but often it leads to further abuse as mentioned
above.

For some women where the abuser was a close family
member there may be a tendency to overvalue or idealise
men rather than be angry or fearful of them. There is a
need to recapture the 'specialness' of the relationship
and, if the abuser was her father, to experience the 'good
Daddy'. If her experience as a child was that sex and
affection overlapped she may sexualise all her relationships with men. This overvaluing of men and the importance
of being close to them concedes to men a great deal of
power and increases the risk of further sexual exploitation.

Many survivors believe they will always be mistreated
by men. They continue to enter abusive relationships as

adults as a form of self-punishment because they believe they were to blame for the abuse. This also keeps them in the role of victim. The negative feelings which character-ise such relationships confirm for her the belief that she is worthless, unlovable and so on. In this situation, survi-vors are recreating the patterns of their family of origin and the whole experience feels very familiar.

Relationships with women may also be difficult for the survivor. She may view women as dependent, weak and ineffectual, and unable to stand up to men. If this is how she views herself and other women it is not surprising that she is unable to appropriately express her anger towards men, with the result that the hostility may be expressed towards women or herself. This can prevent the survivor from creating the kind of relationships with women which might give her the support and nurturing she needs. If she can not trust or value women, is unable to make friendships with them and finds men emotion-ally unavailable, she is unable to find any relief from the feelings of isolation.

This highly negative view of women can result in the survivor only seeing women as important when they become rivals for the attention and affection of men. This can bring problems if the survivor has a daughter. She may become convinced that the very situation she fears – abuse of her daughter – is inevitable.

Her anger towards women can also mask her longing for a relationship with a caring woman. Some survivors have consciously experimented with lesbian relationships in order to have a loving and caring relationship without emotional or sexual exploitation.

For some, relationships with women are important, as Carole says: 'I have always had good relationships with women and have been lucky with the people I have chosen as friends. They have always been more important to me than my family because my family was never there for me.'

Survivors may become prostitutes, believing that if sex is all they are good for they might as well be paid for it, and have sex in a situation they can control. For others, prostitution is the result of needing to have many sexual partners to confirm that they are OK. Repeat victimisation can be a hard pattern to break but, as Donna has shown, it is possible to begin.

Healthy relationships are difficult for anyone to achieve. Inevitably, as you read through these chapters you will be assessing your current relationships and learning to discriminate between who is abusive and who is not. You might find yourself wanting to weed out those who hurt you, minimise you or discount you in favour of those who listen, care and try to understand. Be aware of your feelings after seeing a particular person – if you feel negative, angry, or depressed this person might not be good for you. Notice the difference in how you feel when you are valued and listened to.

During your healing you will be changing in many ways and this will effect the way you relate to other people. Your partner may feel the amount of feelings and changes are too frightening, and put overt or covert pressure on you to stay as you are. You may have to let go of the destructive people in your life as there is no guarantee that they will change with you.

Intimacy

'Intimacy is a bonding between two people which is based on trust, respect, love and the ability to share deeply. You can have intimate relationships with lovers, partners, friends or family members. Through these relationships you experience the give-and-take of caring'*

'I've been married three times – I don't tell many people that.' *Sue*

Problems with intimacy are almost universal for survivors. The child's experience of betrayal, loss of power and control, inability to trust and feelings of low self-esteem are reflected in her adult relationships. Fear of further

* 'The Courage to Heal' Laura Bass and Ellen Davis, page 223

betrayal and abandonment prevent her from taking risks in her closest relationships. There is confusion about who to trust because she can not be sure her judgements about other adults are accurate. She is unsure of how to set up limits and boundaries within adult relationships, and of what they should be. Her inability to protect herself within a relationship may lead to avoidance and continued isolation.

It is understandable that women who have memories of being abused and controlled by men, often through threats or actual violence, may find their fears of men remaining even when they are on an apparently equal footing. Survivors who feel particularly let down by their mothers may find forming close relationships with women difficult – their view of women will be that of their mother – they are dependent, weak and of no use, so few friendships are made where there is total openness and intimacy.

Some women long to be able to be dependent and protected, but fear giving away the emotional control and independence which has kept them safe. This can result in difficulty in expression of real feelings and attracting emotionally unavailable partners to avoid breaking down the barriers. Relationships are often kept brief to avoid intimacy. As with the abuse experience, women may believe their partner is giving emotionally, but discover in reality that they are only wishing to gain sexually. This can cause feelings of disillusionment and loss to resurface. Survivors may repeat the pattern of their childhood, trying hard to please their partners and denying their own feelings and needs, developing an apparently close relationship but never experiencing real intimacy.

Remember the child has made logical assumptions based on what she is told and experienced. In adulthood this may be confusing, particularly for example if someone does not want sex from you (as people did in the past). The feeling of confusion and possible rejection comes from the perceived 'value' placed on sex and the misplaced assumption that 'if they don't want that then I am worth nothing'.

It is not unusual for women's attempts to become intimate to lead to physically or sexually abusive relationships. Their childhood experience leaves them believing they have no rights or choices, which allows other to take advantage of them. Difficulty in recognising their own emotional needs, accompanied by an inability to protect or assert themselves, means they are open to violation.

Some survivors will have married very young to escape the abusive family, but it is likely that problems of trust and intimacy will be a feature of their new relationship.

Sexuality

'I find it hard touching my partner and I am not keen on him touching me so love making isn't easy.' *Sue*

Of her first marriage, Sue says: 'Our marriage was good but sex was a duty to perform. I knew then that I was different. I wasn't getting anything out of it, not like it was meant to be. Love and sex should be wonderful and special – not for me. I would do anything to get out of it. It was dirty and messy. I didn't like it, but still I became pregnant – amazing really. Our marriage lasted seven years – not bad considering. Poor Fred didn't really understand me, so he found someone warmer who was able to offer him comfort and love. Afterwards, I dated again but still couldn't feel anything – I didn't know why.'

'Until my husband taught me how to relax I had never had an orgasm and always felt sex is payment for a good night out with a man. Luckily, I know different now, but I had a reputation as a teenager. I thought sex was the only way to show love.

'I don't like my body and can not imagine why my husband fancies me. I feel fat and frumpy. I don't like him just touching me on impulse as it makes me feel cheap. He can't understand this but to me it means so much.' *Tracy*

For some women, the more emotionally intimate they are with their partner the less sexually intimate they become. This may be because the sexual side of the relationship has become a routine or duty, which was how the abuse was experienced. For other women, there is a sense of losing the ability to control the relationship if emotional dependency has developed, and a belief that the person will be able to hurt them if any form of need is expressed.

Sex may be mistaken for intimacy because as children sexual activity may have been surrounded by a tenderness and gentleness never shown at other times. The experience of sex has been so contaminated for survivors that they may miss out on the intimacy which can be experienced through loving, caring, sexual contact.

Some survivors only experience flashbacks when a certain level of intimacy is reached. Fear of triggering these prevents women from continuing any relationship which might give the emotional support and nurturing they seek. For others, becoming emotionally involved brings sexual difficulties – they can only be aroused sexually and experience pleasure when there is no emotional involvement at all. This presents problems as they are compelled to have relationships with those who are going to confirm their negative beliefs about themselves.

The issue of power and control is always present in abuse. For some, this is experienced as an inability to say 'NO' to their partner, and is accompanied by feelings of helplessness and resentment. They may feel taken over, possessed by their partner, and feel they are again experiencing loss of identity and a blurring of boundaries. Other women equate sexual desire with fear because they think they will be unable to use their power appropriately and will exploit others as they were exploited.

Donna says: 'Sex used to be my outlet but not so much now. To have an orgasm means losing control – I would never have one. I won't let go during sex. I think I once let go and shocked myself so much that I haven't done it since – how dare I lose control. Sex is something I know I can really control. I can not change a lot of things which happen to me but I can change that – I can control it. To lose that control would mean losing quite a bit.'

For others the experience has taught them they can have power through sexuality and validate who they are. They have learnt they can use sexuality to obtain attention and love – that was their experience of close relationships as a child and they don't know anything else. For most women the abuse has a negative effect on their adult sexuality. Children are sexual beings, but to be forced to become sexually active before they are naturally ready will have an effect on their sexuality. For many, this stems from the physiological arousal they experienced during the abuse, which can be thought of as a 'betrayal' of the body. Trust in their body is lost when strong negative feelings are accompanied by physical pleasure.

After a period of time the child's body will respond to the touch. This is normal – it means the body is working properly. These natural body reactions are often distressing – the child might even orgasm. As a child your body will have responded even if your mind did not want it to. One author used the following analogy to explain: 'being physically excited is the equivalent of laughing when you are tickled – you don't necessarily want to but you can't help it'. Forgive your body for reacting in the way it did – this type of arousal is different from the arousal we experience as adults which depends not only on physiological stimulation but also on our thoughts and feelings.

For some survivors their experience results in a lack of sexual desire, even in close, loving relationships. This may result from feeling ashamed or guilty when desire was first experienced because as a child sex was bad, frightening, secret and so on. Sexual desire can lead to the feeling that as a sexual being you were therefore responsible for the abuse, and some women may feel sexual desire as identification with the abuse.

Other women may only be able to experience sexual desire if they have total control over the sexual encounter. They need to be the hunter and are only interested in attracting men who have not made the first move. This may lead them to repeat having relationships with men who are not really interested in them, and who are emotionally unavailable and often abusive.

One of the main problems in experiencing sexual arousal is the ability for it to produce flashbacks to the abuse. These may be fleeting images or an intense memory accompanied by sensory experiences, and may be triggered by a certain touch or smell, which can produce fear, anxiety and an inability to continue with love making. Once a woman has had such an experience it can block her desire for further sexual contact for fear that the experience will be repeated. This can make her feel guilty that her anxiety is preventing her from becoming aroused and she is, therefore, creating difficulties for her partner. Even if you do not experience flashbacks you may still experience a feeling of panic resulting from the abuse and a sense of having 'been there before.'

There are many other reasons why survivors find sexual arousal threatening. The loss of control can lead to a fear of being vulnerable to your partners needs and desires, and of not having the ability to protect yourself. You may fear making noises because you were told to be secret and silent.

Arousal may be experienced as more shameful than desire because it is felt the desire should be ignored and not allowed to lead to a situation where arousal results. Feelings of shame can also result from being seen by your partner to enjoy sexual activity. You may be able to let your body respond and experience sexual arousal, but you find you become emotionally detached from the experience.

If you have experienced sexual arousal during the abuse, orgasm may bring with it feelings of guilt. For some women orgasm, is achieved but not associated with pleasure, and for many the ability to reach orgasm is determined by how much they trust their partner and how safe they feel to lose control.

Survivors who experienced violent abuse may find they can only experience arousal an orgasm if it is associated with violence, either actual physical aggression or violent fantasies during sexual activity. This can be confusing and frightening, but it is not determined in any conscious way – it was the way you were taught by those who had control over your body. As a child, the violence became linked with the normal physiological response to sexual stimulation. Similarly fantasies can be experienced involving the abuser or children being abused, which may lead to feelings of guilt and shame.

Women may be aware of their lack of interest in sex, which can be a symptom of depression or a reluctance to have physical contact. Some women find relief in becoming pregnant and being able to justify ceasing intercourse. Others are motivated to have sex but experience physical symptoms which make it difficult, such as vaginismus, where the outer muscles of the vagina contract involuntarily to prevent penetration. Survivors may also experience vaginal or pelvic pain, often caused by tension and anxiety, though it can result from damage through the abuse. Constant bouts of vaginal infection or thrush are often experienced with little relief from medication. For women whose partners do not know about the abuse find these unexplained difficulties create tension and confusion. Lack of interest or constant physical symptoms which prevent sexual intimacy can be see as rejection of the partner.

Parenting

'I was too protective as a parent' *Anon*

'When my children were ill I was terrified – the responsibility was frightening. I didn't think I was capable of taking proper care of them. Ian had gastro-enteritis when he was about eight months old and I was convinced he was going to die.' *Carole*

For some survivors the decision to have a baby can be a difficult one, they may be aware of the lack of nurturing they received and wonder if they have the ability to satisfy a child's emotional needs. For some, the fear of being a potential abuser is too great to overcome, while others fear they could not have a 'normal' pregnancy or baby.

Survivors who wish to have children may be fearful of having a boy baby. Sue says: 'I never wanted a baby boy. Thank god I didn't. It might sound daft but the very thought of having to change a nappy on a boy baby – to touch him – I would have found it quite repulsive, I don't know what I would've done. I might have coped. While I was pregnant my sister and sister-in-law were pregnant and both had daughters. I thought – daft as it might seem – 'I hope I have a boy because they will be pleased that I could produce a boy – they wanted a boy – and they'll like me.' But I didn't want one. The only reason why I wanted one was so Mum and Dad might like me because I had something different. When I had L. I was glad she was a girl, and definitely when I had M. – I would have gone crazy if I had a boy then.'

For some the thought of having a girl is just as difficult: 'I was dreading having a girl and now I have three. I dread anything happening to them. I feel over-protective of my girls but I think that is good. My children have never experienced any form of sexual abuse and I hope my ability as a watchful mum means they never do.' Tracy

Some survivors find it difficult to touch their children. They are unclear about boundaries between sexual and non-sexual touch, which can make the every day care of small children a time of deep anxiety. Many women are conscious that they treat their son differently to their daughters – they feel a coldness and reluctance to be physical with the male child. For Donna, this extends to her grandson as well as her son: 'When you have children it is hard. When my son was little I was a normal mum – I could cuddle him and when he fell down I would pick him up. When he turned ten years old he was very big and I couldn't go to him if he fell down to hug him. He was always a softy when it came to things like Lassie and would cry his eyes out. I would have to walk away. I could not cuddle him. Now, if he comes near me I flinch and have to stop myself from pulling away. I have to think to myself 'he is your son, don't be stupid.' He gave me a hug on Mothers Day last year and

I just froze. I don't know if it is because he is becoming a man or because he is my son, but at the back of my mind I'm thinking that if it happened to me I could do it to him, so I pull away. I thought this was just me being a cold hearted, bad mother, but when I found out from another girl that she had done exactly the same it went into perspective for me. He doesn't say anything to me about it – he's 20 now. He must have noticed it when he was younger. If he asks I will tell him but I wouldn't openly say this is the reason why I do this. I left the books hanging around and told him I was sexually abused and left him to deal with it, but he hasn't asked me any questions. I am not very close to my grandson. I worry about what will happen when he reaches 12 – will I do the same thing or am I going to over-compensate for it and treat him differently? It would be wrong to treat him differently to how I treated my own son. When I go out with him I say he is my grandson but I don't want to get close to him. It is hard to explain but because his father is my son I don't want to show my son I have those feelings for the baby because I don't have them for him. It is not really a conscious thing. I hold him for a few minutes and give him back. His other grandmother cuddles him the whole time and can't wait to get her hands on him. I can't wait to put him down – quickly.'

In some incidents a son reminds the women of their abuser – he may look physically similar if the abuser was a close relative, and this cause strong feelings of confusion and guilt. In Carol's case: 'It got worse. The nightmares I was having about the abuse didn't have the abusers face they had my sons face – so by the time he was 14 I had totally withdrawn from him. I couldn't bring myself to put my arm around him or touch him in any way. He knew something was wrong and now he says I changed towards him at exactly the time I did, but he doesn't know why. The only contact we really had was joking – everything was non-meaningful. He now lives with foster parents, as does the younger one. They have different foster parents as they never kept in touch and are so different – they don't even know each other. They are both happy though, and that is all I ask for. They can't trust me to give them the love I withdrew, and when I was ready to give that love after my healing things had gone much too far and they were not prepared to trust me. I must earn that trust, and I fully intend to, a bit at a time. By letting them both go I am hoping they will grow up in a stable family background, which both foster parents provide, and will have the chance to start their adult lives on a much better footing than myself. I love them dearly – I think they both know that deep down inside and I keep telling them, so I hope they know.'

Survivors are often aware of the impact their experience has had on their parenting skills. Having had parents who did not protect or care for them, they consider themselves more sensitive and responsive to the needs of their own children, and are often over-protective, especially toward daughters. Sue says: 'I was probably obsessive about cleanliness – 'you must wash between your legs, you must have a bath everyday! I was daft about washing and cleaning – obsessive about cleaning the house. It really wrecks your life. You become paranoid about everything.'

Some women feel a constant sense of danger when their daughters are not close by them, and are unable to let anyone else, even their partner, care for them.

Survivors may doubt their ability to be 'good' mothers, and if they are struggling to deal with the problems resulting from their experience they may feel they are too depressed or anxious to give their children the time and nurturing they need. They may place too much emphasis on the practical and physical side of parenting, wanting their children to be 'clean and tidy' but unable to relax and enjoy simply 'being' with them. They perceived their own mothers as weak and ineffectual, so they may blame themselves for everything which is painful or difficult for their own children. Often the survivor as a child, or later as a parent herself, models how her own parents should have looked after her.

As Carole says: 'I still think I haven't been a very good mother, though my children don't agree – they think I've been OK. I wanted to be a better mother than the one I had. I don't think my mother was taught how to do it, which is, perhaps, why she couldn't help me. It never occurred to me to abuse my children. I love them to bits, even though I wasn't sure I wanted to be a mother at the time. Ian was an accident and Lynne wasn't, but even then I wasn't sure that I wanted another child. Brian did, though, very much. I didn't mind what sex the children were but I was pleased to have a son and a daughter. They are very different people – Ian was an angelic child, never a moments trouble, and Lynne was a handful at times – but though they needed different handling I didn't love one more than the other. They have grown up to be really nice people. I wish I had spent more time with them when they were small instead of worrying about the housework and other superficial things.'

Parenting may not present too many problems while the child is small but when they begin to become sexually mature the mothers feelings may change. Some women struggle to cope with their son's development.

Carol speaks: 'I was fine when the boys were younger, but when J. reached 11 or 12 I was terrified of him – I had nightmares, and he replaced the abuser in those nightmares. I withdrew from him and replaced my love with material possessions – now he's got problems.'

For women whose childhood has been taken away from them there is the danger of trying to relive that childhood through their children. They may try to impose their 'fantasy childhood' on their own child, creating a childhood experience they longed for – giving them what they did not receive, wanting them to achieve what they were unable to achieve. Women may then find themselves resenting the experience they have wanted so desperately for their child, asking themselves, for example, why the child should have such a good relationship with the father, or feeling jealous of their daughter's relationship with their partner. Though the parent part of the woman's personality is doing the best for her child, they have as a result activated the feelings of their own inner child, so the actual child and their inner child compete for the nurturing they both need.

Where abuse was experienced within the family there may be problems in dealing with relationships: guilt at preventing family members from having contact with children, or difficulty coping with the fear when around those who perpetrated the abuse or failed to protect the survivor.

The experience of pregnancy can re-awaken feelings related to the abuse. Some women feel 'taken over', no longer in control of their bodies, which reminds them of the loss of control they experienced during the abuse. For some women, the fact that they are seen as obviously sexual because of their pregnancy brings up feelings of guilt and shame, while for others it brings a relief that they are no longer sexually 'available'. Some women enjoy their pregnancies because they receive the nurturing they need from their partners while having a reason to receive it without sexual contact.

For some survivors the medical aspects of pregnancy are difficult to cope with, particularly internal examinations which can trigger flashbacks or intense emotional recollections. Survivors may find sexual intercourse difficult during pregnancy, fearing that the baby may be damaged by what seems like an incest experience, having their partners penis so close to the baby.

Childbirth may bring memories of the abuse, triggered by a feeling of being out of control in a sexual situation. Some women may find it difficult to accept labour which has not been straightforward, believing their bodies have betrayed them again. Childbirth can also trigger the first recollection of the abuse.

Survivors may have confused feelings about breastfeeding. They may be unable to breastfeed because they have learned to distrust non-sexual sensual touch. For some it can seem too sexual and they fear their own arousal, which seems like a betrayal of their body and an act of abuse by them towards their baby. Breastfeeding can bring up feelings of 'ownership' – whose body is this? For those who feel disassociated with their bodies there is not an inability to make the emotional connection between their body and the baby. Others may welcome the chance to feel close to another without involving sexual activity.

Some survivors find the experience of pregnancy and childbirth particularly rewarding because it brings a sense of being 'normal' and feeling powerful as a woman.

Memories

Many survivors have lived through years of having no memories of the abuse. Children who have been wounded in such a terrible way block out the trauma from their memory so as not to recall the pain of the experience.

Often the child victim can not deal with the effects of abuse because she is too close to it. It is often years or decades later before a survivor can feel distanced enough and safe enough to negotiate the experience. Donna's memories began to come back only after her mothers death and when she was many thousands of miles away from her homeland. Only then could she let down her protective guard. It is generally the case that memories are only released and remembered when the woman is ready and able to cope with them. Up till then the survivor may have a strong feeling that something is not 'right' but not be able to put words to the feeling.

They dissociate, or cut off, from the experiences and feelings which threaten to overwhelm them, not having any conscious memory of the abuse. This also alleviates feelings of guilt.

The incidents are often forgotten because the abuse was hidden. By keeping it secret the child sees herself as an accomplice, which leads her to feel guilty and ashamed. These experiences will often be cut off from the memory. It is normal to block out memories which are too painful, as it is a way of protecting ourselves from a situation which is too difficult to handle with the skills we have at the time. The memories are there, but hidden in the sub-conscious, and your behaviour may offer clues – you fear the dark, or as with Donna, you fear old people. As a child, forgetting was your way of protecting yourself. It was your means of survival.

Some women can not remember anything about their abuse and function reasonably well in adulthood. At some time they may remember because memories can often be triggered by an important life event – the birth of a baby, death of a family member, personal success or failure – where we have strong feelings which were also associated with the abuse. Initially, memories may be vague – an unfocused idea that something happened but with no details. Sometimes, many memories become condensed to form one memory which appears to be of a single event, and it is not unusual for women in therapy to discover that the first incident of abuse occurred at a much younger age than they at first remembered.

Many survivors are anxious to remember all the details of the abuse, but it is important to recognise that we do not remember all the details of any childhood incident, no matter how traumatic, and for those survivors who experienced abuse on a regular basis trying to remember every event would be like trying to remember what you did in every playtime at school. It is always difficult to remember in detail events which happened a long time ago, and to protect us our subconscious only allows as much as we can cope with to enter our conscious awareness.

Carole could remember a great deal of her childhood and when she started to tell her story in the safe environment of therapy more and more memories came back to her, sometimes in nightmares.

There are many triggers which may provoke memories. Here we present a list of the most common:

    death of a parent
    commitment to an intimate relationship
    struggles with an authority figure

children/pregnancy
invasive surgery
physical illness
abandonment
sex
smell and other sensory stimuli
death of abuser
change in life circumstance
promotion or inheritance
learning self defence
becoming physically fit
admission to a psychiatric hospital
start of a sexual relationship
rape
miscarriage
abortion
films/media
other person disclosure

Though freeing the memories will help you make connections between your childhood experiences and the way you function as an adult, and will help integrate the different parts of your life by providing missing pieces of information, each released memory will be accompanied by the feelings you had at the time. This can be very painful but it is important to remember you now have adult ways of coping with those feelings. The memories can never be as bad as the original event – you now have the power and control. Once you become aware of the situations or behaviours which trigger the memories, you can avoid them until such time that you decide you will face them. You can tell someone what is happening to you, ask for their support and let them know exactly what you will need to help you at such times.

Donna finds it difficult to sleep at night because she re-experiences the feelings and sensations of someone touching her when she is in bed in the dark. Her way of coping as an adult is to work from 10 pm until morning; then she can then sleep undisturbed during daylight.

Medical procedures can often bring back memories of sexual abuse. In a paper by J Kitzinger* she describes an incident recounted by a member of the nursing staff: 'We were catheterising an old blind woman; she must have been about 90. It took four nurses to carry out the procedure – three of us were needed to hold her down. And all this old woman was saying was: 'please don't do it Daddy, please don't do it Daddy.' We were all silent. It was never discussed, nobody dared mention it.'

Invasive medical procedures can cause flashbacks. Sue was reluctant to surrender her body to the doctor – survivors often avoid putting themselves in a powerless position – and she now prefers to be seen by a woman. The same can happen with visits to the dentist; for women who have experienced being forced to perform oral sex, lying back in a dentist's chair can cause flashbacks.

Many survivors experience flashbacks in which they re-experience the original abuse. These are vivid, usually visual, images which throw the woman back into her past. The woman is taken right back to the child's experience, with all the vividness and feelings endured then. When this happens the images are accompanied by all the feelings she experienced at the time, and may result in her acting in the same way as she did as a child, reacting in ways which 'protected' her – assuming a foetal position, holding her breath, counting backwards, mentally withdrawing from the situation and so on. For some survivors, flashbacks are experienced like a series of slides, from which they are emotionally detached, being flashed on to a screen. They can be observed without the original sensations or responses. They can be a terrifying experience for the woman, and can seem real in every sense.

Some form of flashback is almost always experienced by survivors, and though visual flashbacks are more common they can involve a wide range of experience from all

* *Nursing Times*, January 17 1990, Vol 86, No 3

senses – visual, auditory, smell, taste and even physical sensations.

Donna recounts her experience: 'Dreams didn't happen until I was an adult. They were dreams but they weren't dreams. I had no dreams of anybody touching me. All I had was an image of someone being in the bedroom and the bedclothes being pulled away, and no matter what I did those bedclothes would move. I would wake up and still feel the bedclothes moving. It is so vivid it is not what I call a dream. You don't wake up and think 'oh that was a dream'. You wake up and you are petrified. It hasn't happened since I moved here but if I got really uptight and worried I would feel it. Then I'd have to get out of bed and go downstairs. I couldn't stay in the bedroom.

When it first came to light I lived in a brand new flat and everything was brand new in it. I moved that bedroom around I don't know how many times – I just couldn't sleep in it. As soon as I went to sleep the bedclothes would move and I would have this image of someone standing at the side of the bed. That is what started me working nights, because I sleep in the mornings – when it came to daylight I could go to sleep, so I just took a night job. It happens more if you are uptight. Work is the only way I can shut off and just get on and do something else. I do my work at the garage all night and then go to a cleaning job, and I have to make sure I am really tired otherwise I won't go to sleep. I don't go to bed now until 1 or 2 pm – most people who work nights finish at 6 am, and are in bed by am and up at 1pm. I would go nuts if I did that. I have to be so tired that I block everything out.'

Flashbacks may occur at a time of symbolically related events – while feeling out of control, experiencing a loss – or by everyday events – hearing a certain piece of music, a tap running, a particular smell, or being touched in a certain way.

In the process of healing it is important to expect and prepare for flashbacks and ultimately gain control of them. You may not be able to speak, or in some cases move, while experiencing them, but you are safe now. When you are experiencing flashbacks know that they are a normal response for someone who has endured abuse as a child. Survivors often describe seeing or hearing things associated with the abuse which are disturbing and out of their control. Shapeless, shadowy figures are often described as being seen during the day or night, usually in a place associated with the abuse. They may appear as evil or menacing, and trigger panic attacks. It is not unusual for all or parts of a partner's body to be replaced with that of the abuser, especially during sexual activity.

Many women describe hearing sounds which are associated with the abuse – the abuser calling their name, particular music or a clock ticking for example. This does not always occur during sex but may happen at any time. Some survivors describe feeling being touched on the face or body, or feeling someone breathing on them. They may sometimes feel the presence of another person in bed.

A survivor may feel she is going crazy – Sue says 'I felt I was going crazy at times', and Carol says 'I have thought I was going crazy many a time' – or feel there is something wrong with her, but flashbacks are a way of helping release the hold the past has over the present. By talking about the details the pain and the emotional intensity of the flashbacks will diminish.

Recovery of memories is important, but what is more important is dealing with the effects of the abuse on how you think and feel about yourself – undoing the damage to your self esteem, your relationships and the ways you have developed to cope. You do not have to remember to heal from the past, but as you begin to heal it is likely that more memories will come back, because part of your healing will have been developing the ability to cope with them.

The abuse experience may cause a loss of faith. In some situations this will happen because a member of the church was directly involved, or because religion is associated with family hypocrisy. As a child, images of a loving protector of little children who is letting you suffer may further confirm that you are 'bad' or lead to outright disbelief in God's existence. For some women their belief in a higher entity brought comfort to them as children – a person who could share their secret and, as an adult, an accepting, loving figure.

Survivors may struggle with the notion of forgiveness when expressing their faith – spiritual counselling will often focus on the need to forgive the abuser before you can heal.

False Memory Syndrome

There has been much debate in the media recent weeks and months regarding a theory developed by Psychologists in America known as 'False Memory Syndrome'. It is claimed that children can create 'false memories' to 'please' adults who question them. This has subsequently led to controversies about how children are interviewed and the accuracy of the evidence they supply. As a result of this work adults undergoing therapy, recalling abuse experienced years beforehand, have also been accused of presenting 'false memories'. Organisations have been set up both in America and in Britain by parents who say they have been falsely accused by their adult children of sexual abuse. The claims are that memories of abuse can be induced or suggested during psychotherapy sessions.

As we have seen through the women's stories in *Betrayal of Trust* burying the memories is often the child's only way of coping with the trauma of abuse, leaving the adult woman with indicators that things are not all right, for example nightmares, illnesses, sexual difficulties and so on. Retrieval of memories is a slow and painful process – often accompanied by strong feelings and physiological responses.

As far as we are concerned the idea of False Memory Syndrome is purely a defensive response to the breaking of secrecy by many people who have suffered abuse.*

* One would expect abusers to quickly latch onto any theory, organisations, etc, which protect their position

Judith Herman, Associate Clinical Professor of Psychiatry at Harvard Medical School, quoted in the *Sunday Times,* 20th June 1993 said 'It has taken 20 years for women's organisations to bring the enormity of sexual assault to public attention. As more victims try to hold their abusers accountable it is natural to expect a backlash.'

If we look back to the World of the Child we can see that the mechanisms for keeping the child quiet are being used to keep the adult from talking.

Any survivor will know on some level the reality of her experience, but will often need the safety of therapy to retrieve her memories.

Dreams and Nightmares

'Dreams are letters from the unconscious, nightmares are telegrams'*

Dreams and nightmares are another way of reaching our unconscious memories and connecting our past to the present. One author calls them the 'windows to our self'†

During waking hours it is possible for our conscious awareness to be defended to protect us from memories from the past. During sleep we may be troubled by our subconscious reliving or reworking of those memories.

For some women nightmares are the first step in recovering memories, while for others they may occur once the woman has begun to disclose the abuse.

The content of nightmares may vary, but the themes which run through them seem to have a commonality. They may include scenes of death or harm to yourself, a child or those close to you, or they may involve being trapped or pursued. For some women they are terrifying because they contain horrific images of violence, bloody and threatening. Whatever the content, they are accompanied by acute emotional reactions – fear, distress and, at times, physical pain.

* Calof D UK Training Workshop, 1988
† M J Williams *Hidden Memories*, 1991, Health Communications Inc

Sometimes, certain incidents or aspects of the survivor's experience are repeated. The abuser may be present but often his identity is hidden or changed.

Carol says: 'The nightmares got worse – in those I was having about the abuser the abuser's face had my son's face, so by the time he was 14 I had totally withdrawn myself from him.'

Occasionally, survivors have 'night terrors' which occur at a deeper level of unconsciousness and may not be remembered, but at this level the woman has the ability to move her body. She may scream, cry, hide, try to escape from the room or hit out at those who try to approach her. Once she has woken from the terror she may be shocked and upset for many hours.

For Sue the need to escape during such experiences put her life at risk. 'I had nightmares until I had been through the group. They were always the same, involving a bus coming towards us and me protecting my husband. I remember dragging him out of bed saying 'quick, you've got to get out of bed'. There would always be this bus coming and I would jump out of the way to escape it. I went through the window a couple of times. I pushed my hands and head through. I had to get out. It was terrible. I think I was asleep and the noise and shock woke me. The worst time was when I went head first. I put my head through it – I really wanted to get out and probably by banging my head woke myself up. I remember going to bed but can not honestly say I was feeling uptight. I used to sleepwalk as a child, and even as an adult I still did it. Each time it happens I am trying to get away. If we ever go anywhere to stay, even now, I always make sure I'm not near the window. If there is a window I put a chair or something near it so I'm going to hit the chair and wake myself up. It was really terrifying.'

Children often experience 'bad' dreams or nightmares, and are fearful of the dark or of going up the stairs at night. For women, often with children of their own, these experiences are harder to accept and deal with.

Survivors can begin to take control of their nightmares

by replaying them when they wake up. They can change the outcome so they turn and face the attacker, or bring in a strong controlling adult to protect them. In the case of a recurring scenario it may help to write down the new ending and read it to yourself before you fall asleep.

For Carole, her dreams and nightmares were excellent indicators of where she stood in her healing process. Understanding helped guide her healing. They showed how she was hurt and how she could help herself. They showed her with simplicity and explicitly how she had everything she needed for healing and that she was heading in the right direction. They also helped her reconnect with parts of her personality from which she had become parted – mostly her inner child (discussed later in the book) and connect her past to her present.

Sometimes, the symbolism was clear, as in the following two dreams:

'I was talking to my mother and we were standing at a dressing table. It had one large mirror and two adjustable side ones. We did not look at each other directly but held our conversation while both looking at each other through the mirrors.'

'I was going down into a cellar. The steps were stone and the cellar dark and damp. The steps were wet. It was so dark at the bottom I could not see anything at all. Suddenly a huge, black door opened, bringing in the light and providing a way to escape.'

Two important indicators of how far Carole had shaken off the ties of her father were the following: 'I had gone to the house of someone I knew from Sunday school to tell him about what was happening at home. I was taken to a very light room where I saw a stack of shelves. The shelves were full of large ornaments – jugs, jars, bowls and figures. They were all pink except one which was the head of a man and was black. I then realised my grandmother was in the room. After a while my father arrived. I had my back to him and I heard him tell me I had to leave with him. He was very angry. My grandmother supported him and also said I had to leave. I was frightened at that point but when I turned to face him, though the look on his face was dark and angry, I said I was not leaving and wasn't scared of him any longer. I didn't leave. The fear of him which I had had for over 30 years left me completely in the dream and I was shocked and surprised to realise the fear didn't return when I woke up.'

'My father came into my room masturbating, as he often did, telling me what he was going to do with me. In the past it had been impossible to disobey his orders but on this occasion I told him he needn't start all that because he was never going to do that to me again. I felt quite safe and in control of the situation. I was not frightened at all.'

Another dream shows how her inner child was present. 'I was in a very large bathroom. It had one bath in a very light corner of the room and another in a very dark corner. In the dark corner the bath was old and stained, and full of stagnant water. In the water was a body which was lifeless and rotting. everything was dark and depressing. In the other corner, the light corner, was a clean white bath with no water in it – just a beautiful, healthy, clean, happy girl, and she seemed to be bathed in sunshine. Everything was yellow and bright.'

Beliefs

Even though women can see very real indicators of themselves being worthy – they may have achieved in many areas of their lives by gaining a degree, raising a child and so on – their early conditioned beliefs force them to discount their achievements and they continue to believe they are worthless.

Often the hardest belief to change is that she is wholly or partially responsible for the abuse. This can lead to guilt feelings and depressive episodes. Society often supports the idea that the child has in some way colluded with the abuser. 'I must have been seductive as a child' is an idea often expressed by survivors and used as justification by the public. A close male friend of Carole, when told about the abuse, said: 'It must have been because you were a beautiful child'. Carole was able to challenge him and ask him if he would do the same to his little girl.

'I must have been responsible because I enjoyed it' is another belief women find hard to reject, and is one of the greatest sources of guilt.

Changing beliefs is crucial for healing, especially adopting the belief that 'what happened to me was wrong but there is NOTHING wrong with me'.

FEELINGS

Feelings can not hurt you – they are reactions to your experiences and memories. You may experience a range of feelings associated with the abuse, varying from time to time, which may be more intense at certain times. These could include rage, confusion, sadness, helplessness, despair, guilt, inadequacy, fatigue, shame. Survivors often become numb and attempt to block out feelings through drink, drugs, work, sex, food, a striving for others' approval, romance, shopping, television, gambling and so on.*

All feelings can help you, even ones normally thought of as negative. Feeling anger and expressing it can be positive. We often confuse feelings with the behaviours associated with them. For example, anger is confused with violence. For Carole, her fathers anger was always experienced as violence towards another person, so for Carole as an adult it was difficult for her to feel her own anger – she was terrified of becoming violent like her father and losing control.

We can feel overwhelmed by our feelings, believing we will not survive their intensity. All feelings have a beginning, a middle and an end – they do go and when that happens you are left alive not crazy. If you have repressed

* Linda Sanford Strong *At the Broken Places*, p. 69

your feelings you may be scared and surprised by discovering their depth and intensity. Even happiness can feel threatening if it is a feeling you have not been used to. Often the fear is about the feelings not going away or getting out of control, as in Carole's experience.

If you do not feel anything it does not mean you do not feel but that you are out of touch with your feelings. Survival often means pretence and covering up reality. Carole, like many others 'had to' protect others, and hide her feelings and her past, yet at the same time survive each day.

A lot of energy is used to block unresolved feelings and issues. Feelings may be stored in dangerous amounts, leading to small explosions and illness. As Carole says: 'after court I had a lot of boils. I guess it was the badness coming out.' Throughout her life she has experienced other illnesses, some recurrent.

Expression of feelings is a part of healing. 'The expression of feelings is a natural process to be moved through, the feeling of fear leads to protection; the feeling of sadness leads to relief; anger leads to change; while joy leads to pleasure or relaxation'.*

Feelings must be experienced not just intellectualised to be completed. Survivors often remain 'in their heads', appearing strong and out of touch with their emotions, so initially there is a need for them to identify the feelings.

For many women their low self esteem and feelings of isolation result in periods of depression. During these times they may have increased feelings of worthlessness and despair, withdraw further from family and friends, and experience an inner deadness and loss of emotional response, believing life is not worth living.

The seeds of their depression will have been sown in the abusive family environment where no feelings were allowed, where they had no control over their lives or sense of being able to change, leading to helplessness and

* Petruska Clarkson, p. 109.

hopelessness. Depression is often the result of anger turned in on itself.

Dealing with physical symptoms of the effects of abuse does not allow the survivor to change the underlying cause, but getting help for her depressive episodes – depending on whom she approaches — may enable her to explore the reasons for her feelings rather than being given medication to relieve the symptoms. If she is unable to begin this exploration she may continue to live a life of depressive episodes, always feeling an almost subconscious sense of pain which may eventually bring her to kill herself.

Guilt

The absence of self blame in survivors is unusual, and it is often the feeling of guilt which continues to wreak damage on the woman. The adult still perceives the cause of the abuse to be within herself.

Feelings of guilt can begin in a woman's early childhood. Desperately trying to make sense of her world the child perceives that her parents behave in the way they do because she is bad. The adults in her life may set out to encourage this belief. They may accuse the child – 'see what you made me do' and so on. It must be remembered that adults, especially parent figures, are the centre of the child's universe and, therefore, all powerful. The child may attempt to be better or avoid situations, but it never works and never could, so she feels more guilty. So it goes on.

If you ask an adult survivor why she feels guilty, she may not know; all she feels is an all pervasive sense of guilt. As stated earlier, the child will make the best sense she can of a situation, but because of her egocentric thinking she will see herself as responsible. If asked as a child why she felt guilty she may reply 'because I made Daddy do it'.

As children, most victims blame themselves in some way. This can also stem from direct messages from the abuser, or the mother or other adults, or be implied in the way the child is treated – being punished for telling, or taken away from home because of the abuse.

It is important to remember that you were not to blame regardless of how old you were, your position in the family or how much you knew about sex. It was not your responsibility to stop the abuse. Remember also that abusers will always place the blame elsewhere, even when convicted.

You may feel guilty for not telling the abuser to stop, especially if the abuse took place over a long period. As a child you will have believed everything you were told about possible punishments and the consequences you were threatened with. Maybe you didn't tell because you wanted the things with which you were bribed. It is important to realise that in a family which was not protective or safe, any form of attention or caring would be welcomed. If you felt guilty for enjoying initial caresses and attention you must remember it was that which you wanted, not sexual contact. The only physical touch you ever received may have been during the abuse.

You can not simply get rid of guilt – it takes time and a lot of hard work. It is often accompanied by depression, and if the perpetrator placed all the guilt on to you it can be a heavy load to carry. You can begin by challenging your ideas about what happened. Think of a child you know who is the same age as you were then – what are your expectations of that child? Could she really do the things you think you were supposed to have done? List what you have to be guilty about and ask an objective person to say whether you are justified in feeling that way.

Guilt is a very uncomfortable feeling. When held inside it eats away at your self-esteem. Once acknowledged, survivors can find ways of accepting their behaviour by understanding the reasons for it. They can stop 'beating themselves up' and/or dumping their guilt on to other people.

Guilt arises from being caught between the competing demands of your own needs and those of another. It prevents you from getting what you want because you have become accustomed to putting the needs of others first. It can stop you from being aware of your own needs and can create feelings of extreme fear when a need is identified.

Shame

Shame is often confused with guilt, but the two are as different as jealousy and envy. Guilt is concerned more with what a person has done, while shame is concerned with feelings of worthlessness, being different from others, inferiority, a deep sense of isolation and alienation, and intense disappointment with yourself. It is a deeper feeling than guilt.

As we have seen in The World of the Child, the perpetrator will often use or create shame in the victim to stop her from telling. Many survivors have to tackle this feeling somewhere in their healing. There are ways around it, but one of the best is to observe children and build up a realistic idea of how vulnerable they really are. Carole talks of seeing her 30-year-old son sitting on a couch with her neighbour's six-year-old (the age Carole's abuse started) and truly understanding how small and defenceless she herself must have been against her father.

Grief

Incest and abuse result in bereavement.

Survivors suffer many losses throughout their childhood and, ultimately, in adulthood. There is the loss of nurturing and protective parents, of trust in others, of innocence and spontaneity, of control over her body, of sense of self, awareness and intimacy, and, fundamentally, a loss of immaturity.

Survivors may be aware of going through a grieving process similar to that experienced after the death of someone close, or they may experience a sense of despair that the loss can never be resolved. Only by giving up the belief that just one person can repair the pain will you be able to feel your grief and move through it. Even if your abuser tries to remove the pain he has caused he CAN NOT repair what he has done – that is up to you.

Anger

Anger is often a difficult emotion to 'own' and express.

Consequently, it is often displaced on to yourself or your partner. The victim does not experience her anger directly because the feeling is viewed as potentially dangerous. She often will talk in grand terms, believing that if she began expressing her anger it would never stop, saying she would kill the person she was angry with. Anger equates with violence as it did in her original family, so she disconnects her anger or directs it at herself, which is self-destructive.

Carole found it extremely difficult to be angry. As a child she had never learned or seen how it could be used constructively. All she saw was that it could lead to pain. Anger meant uncontrolled, violent outbursts and she feared it in herself and others, but, rightly, she had immense authentic anger inside her. Following healing, she now understands and believes love and friendship do not have to exclude the whole range of emotions at our disposal. She can be angry and people will still love her and not abandon her. She can show her anger in ways which are not destructive. She can begin to listen to her inner world rather than ignore it. One author calls it 'the gift of anger'*

Forgiveness

'It was a tremendous relief to be told it is all right not to forgive, because I'd spent so many years trying to. When you feel it's OK to feel the way you do, it's terrific.' *Carole*

Forgiveness is often used to stop ourselves from dealing with our pain, anger and sadness. It can separate us

* *I never told anyone*, Ellen Bass et al, Harper and Row, 1983

from our feelings. There is often great pressure from those close to us to forgive and forget, which is a way for those people to avoid dealing with the pain and feelings the abuse brings up in themselves. They are often genuine in their wish for you to feel better and believe forgiving means that it can be put behind you, relegated to the past.

Carole describes how others tried to convince her that she should forgive: 'I met someone recently whose religious beliefs supported his attitude about abuse. He suggested that until I could forgive my abuser I wouldn't be able to live with it. He said 'You must forgive – forgiveness is everything Carole – until you forgive you will never be happy'. At the time it gave me a lot of anguish and it made me feel wicked.'

'Not long ago I met a friend who had also been abused and forgave the abuser. She told other women at meetings the only thing to do is to forgive. I said 'bullshit!' If that's what they needed, fine, but I couldn't. I felt I had come a long way in therapy because I would never have been able to say that six months earlier.'

Being told to forgive by others implies that if you were a stronger person or less sensitive you would not have to face your past now. This attitude merely serves to hinder healing.

Healing

Carole

There once was a child called Carole
Whose Daddy was away at war,
And each time he came home on leave
She loved him more and more.

Suddenly her dream came true,
He was home to stay for good.
He loved her and protected her
As every father should.

Then one day those feelings changed
And her love and trust grew dim,
The games they played weren't childish then
And she became afraid of him.

He tortured and abused her,
The shock was truly great,
He deprived her of her childhood
And taught her how to hate.

She thought her mother couldn't know,
How could she and not say?
But now she knows the truth of this,
And the hurt won't go away.

And then there's anger deep and strong
That eats her strength away,
It brings out thoughts she doesn't like
Of wanting him to pay.

Trying to come to terms with this
Has been a long, constant strain,
There just had to be another way
Of coping with the pain.

Then a group was formed
With hope of a sure way out,
It's painful but it's going to work
Of that there's little doubt.

The outcome of this group work
And the thoughts that keep her sane,
Is that one day she'll be free of this
And free to live again.

'I sought help because I knew there was something
stopping me being a 'normal' human being. I was
crying too easily – I had hardly ever cried during the
years of the abuse. I was having nightmares, broken
relationships and a strong feeling that I was a horrible
person. I blamed myself for EVERYTHING. I was unlovable, untrustworthy and useless.

The book *Right to Innocence* convinced me I had a lot
to work out. Individual therapy had stirred things up and
helped me to recognise my need to go further. The group
situation seemed the answer – the last chance I would
have. For me, group therapy was the thing which helped
me realise all the things I've written down. I'm sorry I didn't
do it years ago, but I didn't have the opportunity.

At our first group meeting we were asked to list our
hopes and fears for the future. I desperately hoped to
feel better about myself and my life, but my biggest fear
was that I wouldn't, that when my feelings, fears and
vulnerability were exposed I'd have no control and the
loose ends inside my head would never tie up. I might
even go crazy, going through all the pain and either
feeling worse or no different at all.

But there is a difference, and for the better. I've
learned that I am not unlovable, that I have control over
my own body, my mind and my life, and that being used
and abused was not, is not and never will be normal or
acceptable.

I have learned that I have the right to exist, to say
'yes' or 'no', to be happy and, in personal relationships,
to ask for and expect what I need and want. I have
learned that I don't have to put up with anything less. I
have learned that my feelings actually matter and I
don't have to sacrifice them to be sure of being accepted, liked or loved by others.

Confronting my father was another fear, a fear I wasn't sure I'd ever be strong enough to overcome, but with the help and support of the group it has been done and I am no longer afraid of him. Living without that overwhelming fear is like starting life again.

I know I will never forget. How could I ever forget such savage violation of my mind and body? I have accepted that though it happened it has not made me evil as well. For forty years or more the damage affected my relationships, my children and my entire life, but it doesn't have to any more.

I've learned that it takes courage to heal and I still feel needy, but joining the group realised all my hopes and none of my fears.

I have learnt a lot about myself since joining the group. The 'Going into Therapy' poem I wrote describes exactly how I feel, and how much I've changed and gained, how far I've come in believing that I'm an OK person with the right to have feelings, to say 'no', to be loved and, perhaps to have the relationship I've always wanted and deserved with a man I can love and trust completely. I used to be afraid to be happy in case I had to 'pay for it' later. Sometimes, I still feel like that but not so often. I keep telling myself I deserve to be happy.'

RECOVERY

'I hated myself before healing and was scared of anything new – I liked routine, to know where I was in my life, and liked to have a boyfriend around me all the time to make me feel someone loved me. Now I feel stronger and able to do things without being worried. I know I can be loved for myself and not just for my body, and that I can have nice things. I can give love genuinely now and not expect to get something in return.' *Tracy*

'The major changes I made were being able to talk openly, breaking away from my father, and NOT FEELING GUILTY.' *Sue*

'Before my healing I hated myself. Now I know I am a caring, warm and worthy person.' *Carol*

Healing begins with survival. Recovery is experiencing a fulfilling life which is no longer determined by the patterns laid down in childhood.

Reading this book will give you an understanding of yourself and your family, and how and why the abuse has affected you. In knowledge there is power, the power to overcome those effects. Understanding in itself is not enough – healing includes the painful process of re-experiencing the fear, anger and sadness held for so long by your child within, and learning to trust again.

Sue says: 'The hardest part was finding someone to understand, knowing where to get help at my age'.

Some survivors choose to move through their healing with the help of a therapist – some do not. Others find survivors' groups provide the support and security they need to face the past. Increasingly there are workshops for survivors run by therapists and survivors. For those women who feel safer dealing with the abuse on their own there is an excellent workbook* and a self-help programme†.

There is no set pattern to the process of healing, rather a series of interlocking pieces which, when linked together, provide a foundation for growth and change. Each survivor experiences her healing in a different way and at her own pace. You may find you concentrate on a particular area of healing intensely for a while, and then focus on another area of your life until the time is right to move on. These interlocking pieces include believing what happened and speaking about it to another, understanding you were completely innocent, feeling angry, grieving, learning to trust – yourself and others – getting to know your 'child', and re-evaluating your family and the abuser. For some women, the healing will begin with a crisis period when repressed memories surface. Others will want to disclose to family and friends, or confront the abuser and/or those who did not protect them.

As you move through your life circumstances and events may cause you to re-focus on one area of your healing that you thought you had finished with, this re-cycling of experiences, thoughts and feelings strengthens your ability to change, and allows you to integrate your past in such a way that you can come to terms with your family and the abuser. There will always be problems – nobody's life is problem free – but as you heal you will have more tools to deal with them.

It takes strength and courage to overcome abuse; you need to know that you have both, and remind yourself that nothing can be as difficult to cope with as the original experience. The little child within you will be scared – respect her fear and make the journey as safely as you can.

Jackie says: 'The most difficult part was facing up to the abuse.'

* *The Courage to Heal Workbook*, Ellen Bass and Laura Davis
† *The Right to Innocence*, Beverley Engel

Facing the truth of your experience, recognising the knowledge that your life today is a direct result of your past, discovering basic life decisions, coping mechanisms and defence mechanisms, releasing the pain and anger which have been ignored for so long – all this will ultimately free you, but nothing will stay the same. As Carol said: 'The healing process deeply affected every part of my life. My job went, my relationship and friendships were evaluated, every part was re-evaluated.'

Accepting you have been abused and acknowledging your survival is the foundation stone which all the other 'blocks' build on, is the first step to recovery. As one woman said: 'Its like a volcano. Once the abuse is accepted it is just the beginning – it takes a long time to heal.'

Questioning your past will give meaning to your experience as will asking 'why did he do it?', not to explain or forgive the abuse, or to forgive, but to understand for your own resolution. Understand that you were abused not because of who you were but because he was the person he was and you were just there. Everything you did then and the patterns which exist now are a result of the abuse, not because of you.

Becoming aware of 'the world of the child' provides a context for the abuse. Realising the importance of family dynamics, the social environment and life events brings an understanding that the abuse did not 'just happen'.

Beliefs about ourselves are a result of abuse not shared with others. If we do not share experiences we can not test their validity so our own distorted thinking goes on reinforcing them. We often attribute adult abilities to ourselves as children – choices or power which we did not have then. In our search to make sense of the things which happen to us our child part believes 'I'm worthless and bad'. The message from our parent part may have been 'you deserved it', but our adult thinking can tell us 'you were not to blame'. Once you understand how your family provided the environment for such beliefs to become entrenched you can begin to absolve yourself of any guilt or shame.

Carol says: 'The most important thing I discovered was that no matter what I did I couldn't have had any way out of the situation – knowing it wasn't my fault.'

Focusing on the abuse will release feelings from the past – these feelings of anxiety, guilt, shame, anger or sadness may be perceived as overwhelming. They may be accompanied by nightmares, flashbacks, and physical symptoms. You may fear you are going crazy: it is a normal response and the feeling will not last forever. Expression of feelings that you were never allowed to have, can be immensely empowering. In order for those feelings to be released the defences built up as a child need to be gradually and carefully pulled down. This takes courage, patience, and commitment, and support from others is crucial at this time.

Tracy says: 'My husband went through hell and back during my healing as he shared every emotion I was going through. It was hard and we could have given up many times, but we didn't. I think in many ways it brought us closer because while I was learning he was learning too.'

As you change other things have to change with you. Tracy's husband was willing to change with her, but you may find those close to you feel threatened by the changes they witness. They may be scared for you, anxious that your healing is doing them more harm than good, not realising that expressing many 'negative emotions' is part of a cleansing process. Julia describes the reaction of a close friend: 'She became afraid for me when I was getting in very deep, but she accepted my reassurance that I knew what I was doing.' You can encourage partners or friends to read this book or others which explain the healing process. They can seek help themselves from a counsellor, or join a support group for relatives of survivors.

Some people close to you may see the change as more threatening to them – 'It was very difficult at first with my partner who felt resentful and afraid – it's improving now.' *Julia*

Inevitably some relationships will flounder. As you

begin to feel better about yourself you may realise the quality of you relationship, or the treatment you have received, is no longer acceptable. You may discover you are able to break away from partners who you have needed in the past but who are unable to cope with your developing self-esteem and sense of identity.

During the healing process grieving needs to be done – for the lost childhood, the hurt and humiliation, and for the many times when the hurting child within prevented the adult from enjoying the present. The survivor also has to face the realisation and grief of not having 'good enough' parents.

As you become able to re-interpret your past from an adult perspective you will also be able to reassess the ways in which you deal with the 'here and now'. You will begin to understand why and how you put up with the injustices of the past, and realise you do not have to tolerate similar unfair treatment now. You will become less tolerant of people's behaviour when it does not take your needs or feelings into consideration.

Donna says: 'Now I only do what I want, not what other people want. The biggest change is to be able to say 'no' because I didn't know that big word.'

'I was able to consider myself and put myself first instead of everyone else. I took time to listen to ME after all those years.' *Carol*

Some survivors will want to put their experience behind them once they have completed the major part of their healing. Others will want to share their experience and their healing with others. Some go on to form self-help groups, work on crisis lines or write about their experiences. Others are content to carry on with their lives knowing the abuse will always be a part of them but no longer control them.

Carole through her healing process learned what childhood decisions she had made and on what basis she had made them: for example the lack of knowledge she had as a child, her vulnerability – physically and mentally — and the power of her parents at that time. She learned how to trust her feelings and perceptions as REAL rather than those falsely adopted throughout her life as a result of her need to survive. She interpreted her body signals and did not ignore them anymore. For example we know that when she experiences a bad stomach this often links to her feelings rather than any physical ailment.

Carole now tested out her REAL self and found out for herself that people would still love her for being the person she really was and not the person she thought she had to be. She changed or adapted her basic life decisions which make up her life plan, particularly her basic stance of 'I'm not-OK others are'. She learned to respect the defences created in childhood, for example minimising her own needs, and gradually learned to acquire alternative ways of being as an adult. She could respect her defences; after all they had served her well as a child but restricted her as an adult.

Carole was the only person who could complete the tasks of her childhood and deal with the feelings and experiences from that time. It was unlikely her family would help her in repairing the past. Carole made many changes and continues to do so. She has greater self esteem, better ways of coping with what life throws at her and greater self confidence. She says 'Recently at my boss's house I overcame a situation that eighteen months ago would have completely thrown me. It was realising that out of 6 people sitting round the table I was the only one without a degree or University education. For a moment I felt worried but it didn't last and I think I held my own. I have accepted I am not hopeless at everything. It is a good example of how much better I feel about myself.

INDIVIDUAL THERAPY

'The most important part of my healing was therapy, slow and gentle at first, and the total acceptance by

the therapist. I know I can do and say anything with her and she will keep me safe until I feel ready to fly.'
Julia

'The presence of another human being is vital to the perception of a survivor at the beginning, because her ghost is bound to be extremely frightening'*

For some women to heal it is enough to have their story heard by someone who reacts in a calm, supportive manner. Others need to delve deeper into the feelings and ways in which they are still suffering.

You should seek the help of a therapist only when you feel the time is right. Be aware that those close to you may try to persuade you to seek help so they end up feeling better. It may be difficult for them to cope with the effects themselves or how they impinge on your life.

It is important to find a therapist who is familiar with how abuse can effect a victim and is comfortable with the 'what and how' of the survivor's experience.

The gender of your therapist is important – a female therapist is preferable as you will probably be better able to trust her and feel more comfortable discussing the details of the abuse. There may be times during therapy when feelings about past inadequate relationships can be transferred to your therapist. You may treat her as someone from your past, expecting her to hurt or reject you. However, if you feel you would be more comfortable with a male therapist there are men who are sensitive to the power relations which might arise in such a therapeutic situation.

You may find it difficult at first to form a good relationship with your therapist. Fears you have in making an intimate relationship will be present in your relationship with her. It will take time to build up trust and confidence in her ability to contain your feelings. A good therapist will understand and respect your need to build your

* *Cry Hard and Swim*, J Spring, Virago Press, 1987, p. 96

relationship before you both begin to look at the past and how it has affected you.

Therapy can be hard work; it takes time, motivation and a lot of support. With the guidance of the therapist you may look into your unconscious and expose previously hidden memories. She will be able to help you find ways of coping with and overcoming the fears you may uncover. You will be able to explore the impact of abuse in a way which does not only focus on the symptoms, but provides an understanding of why your current problems are linked to the abuse. Understanding why you developed certain coping mechanisms, and why they were so important to you as a child, will make it easier to replace them with more appropriate strategies or discard them completely.

A good therapist will help you focus on the abuse experience, understand the context in which it occurred, allow your 'child' to express her feelings and re-interpret the abuse from an adult perspective, focus on the areas of your life you would like to change and integrate the abuse experience into your identity.

As you recover, you will be able to release negative feelings, feel good about yourself, say 'no' to others, 'know' what your needs are and how to have them met, experience closer loving relationships and become comfortable with your sexuality.

As Julia says: 'I am finally becoming an adult. Adults have rights – the right to be me, just the way I am.'

GROUP THERAPY

Going Into Therapy

Going into therapy seemed the only way
Of coping with the agony I'd lived with day by
    day,

I entered it with caution, damaged and afraid,

Doubting very much that progress could be made.

For what seemed a lifetime we somehow made it
    every week,
Until at last there seemed some hope of future
    much less bleak,

We learned so much about ourselves and each
    other, too,
Of how strong and brave we were after all we had
    been through.

Love, protection and respect should have been
    there from the start,
But our feelings were discounted and we were set
    apart.

We'd lived with guilt and with neglect, we'd lived
    with fear and shame.
But we learned we weren't unlovable, worthless or
    to blame.

And though we'd been abandoned, bullied and
    betrayed,
Despite it all we have survived, we're free and
    unafraid.

Forgiveness isn't possible, of that I'm very sure,
But his power has gone forever, he can terrorise no
    more.

The process was not painless and the memories are
    still real,
But I know with help and courage it is possible to
    heal.

Carole

'The simple sight of what looked a perfectly ordinary gathering of women, one that could have been picked at random from any city street mirrored back to me, as nothing else could have, that incestuous experience had not put me at one remove from the rest of the human race. No one there was the freakish alien we had, in our secret souls, conceived ourselves to be. This was the very first gift we gave to each other, just by sharing our physical presence'*

> What is most helpful is knowing it's not your fault, that others have unfortunately been in the same situation. You can be helped by talking to and listening to someone else. *Anon*

> I needed help and support from someone who knew why I was feeling as I did and could explain it to me – I found it from my therapist. The group was most helpful. I felt safe and not alone. *Carol*

Therapists run groups where survivors can share and explore the impact of abuse in a non-judgmental arena, a safe place where experiences and feelings can be validated by other survivors, and where the 'child' can be supported by understanding adults. The therapist can guide and support you through your healing, and suggest exercises and strategies for dealing with particular difficulties.

Being part of a group can help reduce the feeling of isolation through realising you are not alone, not the only one to have survived abuse. By having your feelings confirmed by other survivors you can learn to develop trust in your own feelings and understand that they and you are normal. As Tracy says: 'The most useful aspect of my healing was the group meetings I went to – I realised I wasn't the only one, and we are all normal and can learn to live normally.'

Survivors often find it easier to resolve their feelings of shame and guilt within the group. This comes from being able to see that their view of how other survivors behaved in coping with the abuse is different to the way they perceive their own behaviour. By applying adult thinking to another's situation they are able to view their own experience differently.

Cry Hard and Swim J Spring, Virago Press, 1987, p. 147

This was Sue's experience: 'After the group I don't feel as much to blame because now I can look at any child and any adult and see that an adult knows what they are doing and a child is a child. There are times when I feel guilty, but I can say 'no you shouldn't'. When you are at home and living under the same roof as your father you do as you are told – you're brought up to respect him – but how can you when they have done that. Yes, there are times when I feel guilty, but I can now think 'no'. I am not going to feel guilty, because it wasn't my fault.'

Having individual therapy may feel stigmatising, an acknowledgement that there is 'something wrong with me'. For some women it will feel too much like being in the 'patient' role and they may find it difficult to feel equal in the relationship. Group therapy has the potential to reduce these feelings.

Survivors have an extraordinary potential to help each other. They have the ability to be understanding adults and caring parents to the 'child' within other survivors, and, as a group, to provide a support network. For many women this is the first place in which they are able to disclose the details of their abuse and begin to feel their emotions. It is often with the support of other members that they begin to disclose to people outside the group or begin to prepare for confrontation. For Carole the overwhelming feeling was not of guilt or anger but of fear, fear of her father which invaded her thoughts and dreams and prevented her from experiencing intimacy. She explains: 'Fear is so powerful it makes you forget everything except survival and if to survive you have to give in to unreasonable demands, ignore your feelings and remain invisible for as long as you can, then you do that. Only when the fear goes can you allow yourself the luxury of 'owning' your feelings and the knowledge that those feelings matter. Then you can even believe you are lovable at last.

I rid myself of my fear by going into therapy with two excellent therapists and with the support of the self-help group. It was slow and painful but it was worth it. It eventually led to the confrontation with my father which finally helped me heal. It is true that there is no cure, but it is possible to come to terms with an awful past without it spoiling the rest of your life. When the fear left me it was like being reborn – I couldn't have done it on my own.' Linda Sanford in *Strong at the broken places* calls this 'emotional reincarnation'.*

Making relationships is often difficult for survivors. Group therapy provides the opportunity to test out relationships and discover that some people can be trusted to take care of them and their feelings.

Jackie says: 'I began to believe some people were OK to trust.'

Within the group new ways of communicating and developing real intimacy can be tested. Risks can be taken where there is immediate help if it is needed. Some women find the idea of a therapist being present in a group difficult, feeling she represents a professional and, therefore, powerful figure. If she has not experienced abuse herself the survivor may feel she can not relate to the group in the way they need. Self-help groups offer all the advantages of group therapy, support and encouragement – a 'good enough' family to replace the old. They require individuals taking the initiative in their own recovery. Survivors and therapists need to be able to agree on a structure and guidelines for how the group is run to provide safety for each member.

DISCLOSURE

When Carole disclosed her experience for the first time she had exactly the response she had wished for. She had built up a relationship with Gordon over many years and was able to trust him. She says: 'It was hard to put into words but once I made the first statement it was easy. I was lucky – he was on my side from square one.'

* Page 71

During the years when Carole tried to put her past behind her she became close to several men and experienced a variety of responses when she told them she had been abused. 'I told both my husbands but they were unable or unwilling to discuss the abuse. My first husband Brian never wanted to talk about it.' Having told her second husband, his reaction was: ' "I shouldn't go telling people about that if I were you." At the time I thought he was probably right, that it was something I should be ashamed of, but in the back of my mind I didn't see why I should feel ashamed – I didn't do anything wrong.'

One friend tried to justify the abuse, responding with: 'If you were such a beautiful child can't you understand why?' Carole quickly reminded him that he had a beautiful daughter and queried whether that would make it possible for him to abuse her. She says 'It is easy for people to see a situation slightly removed until they put themselves in that situation.'

Another close friend said 'Oh dear, that's a shame'. Carole felt he found it disturbing and could not cope with the information. Another passed it off without saying much. Carole says: 'I find that when you tell men they withdraw. They say it is terrible but you know instantly, or I do now, that they don't want to talk about it. I don't think I have met one man who wanted to know. They didn't discount it – they just didn't want to know how I felt or what I thought. I don't think they could cope. I have thought about these disclosures recently. Maybe men identify themselves with the abuser and find it much more difficult to cope with than women.'

'Recently I have discussed the details with a therapy group. It was a very painful process but has brought me the only peace and freedom from the abuse I have ever known.'

When I went to my aunt and uncle's (she was my father's sister) she was very upset by it all. 'She used to advise me that if I found someone nice who I wanted a relationship with I shouldn't mention the abuse. Part of me thought it would be nice not to have to take it into a relationship but it was a part of me. If someone didn't want to know about the way I am there would be no hope, would there? If I was in a relationship which might develop I would feel I would have to disclose. This is typical of my family taboo – secrets will go away so don't tell.'

'I told my sister-in-law. She listened which is all anyone can do. Somebody who has been abused needs someone who will listen and not pass judgement or put in stupid comments. That is the last thing you need – someone putting in trivial comments. I spoke to another person and their reaction was "never mind". When you are pouring your heart out to someone and they say that you could strangle them – it is never "never mind".' *Donna*

For some women, disclosing to their partner, a close friend, a counsellor or therapist, or within group therapy, is sufficient. Sue says: 'I told my partner about two years ago. I helped out at family planning and often chatted to the doctor there. I came home from talking to her one day and somehow it came up. He said "something happened to you, didn't it?" I said "yes, I was abused", and he said "was it somebody close to home?" I said "yes".'

For others, disclosure to the family of origin becomes a central part of the healing. There is no doubt that disclosing the secret in a family where secrecy has been the maintaining principle can have a powerful effect on both the survivor and other family members.

Disclosure allows the survivor to speak the truth, freeing communication within the family. This may provide her with new insights about her family and their shared history, and may also give permission to other family members to make disclosures. If there are still children at risk from the abuser it removes some of the danger for them.

Disclosure also gives the survivor the opportunity to confront her mother, or whoever it is she sees as failing to protect when she was a child. In families where the father is the abuser, the mother is often made powerless and unable to protect her daughter. He actively undermines the mother-daughter relationship to gain control over the child. Understanding the power relations and family dynamics will not remove the feelings of betrayal and hurt, but it may begin to build the bridge in healing the relationship between the survivor and her mother.

When faced with a disclosure even if they knew or suspected, mothers often feel they have been betrayed by their partner and their daughter. The may respond with outrage, feeling hurt and fearing for the survival of their relationship and support system. If they believe the daughter they have everything to lose and nothing to gain. The mother may initially support the daughter but change their allegiance after threats, pleading and attention from her partner, the abuser.

Ideally, disclosure should only take place when the survivor is strong enough to cope with denial, rejection, verbal aggression and so on – when she does not need confirmation of the truth and does not or fear the consequences of speaking out. Sometimes this ideal is not possible – events may dictate that the survivor discloses without preparation. For Sue, the need to disclose her abuse to others was precipitated by her mother's death, which left her father dependent on her for support and care. She found this difficult but was unable to explain her reluctance to the rest of her family. Her father's falling ill and her fear of having to care for him in her own home provided final trigger.

She said: 'I told all my family as I was fed up with being the black sheep. It wasn't my fault and I was fed up with all of them putting me down. My father went into hospital and the hospital asked me if he could come to stay at our house when he came out, I told them 'no'. They weren't very pleased so I explained why. Then I had to tell my family – no-one was that pleased but I was able to say 'no', perhaps for the first time in my life.'

This ability to say 'no' led Sue to tell her story, to strangers at first, where she received understanding and help, and then to her family, whose response was varied. From her account we can understand how, even as adults, survivors will cope with negative feelings to protect the family.

Sue said:

Eventually, they said we ought to take my father to the hospital, so we took him to casualty. Of course, they started to take his clothes off and I thought 'Oh no! I don't want to touch his clothes'. I didn't, yet I had been washing his clothes which I hated – I really hated hanging his clothes on the line. Then they said they would admit him – I was hoping they would because I knew if they let him out he couldn't go back to his flat and would have to stay with me – so he went into hospital. I can remember thinking 'I'm not going in the ambulance with you' and this was really the turning point for me – I switched off from him.

I went to visit him – he'd been in for nearly a week. The next day the phone rang and they asked me to bring in his clothes. That morning I'd thought they were going to say he can come home with me. I walked into the hospital and said 'I've brought his clothes'. The sister looked at me and said 'he can come home if he's got someone to go to – he says he can stay with you'. I said 'he's not coming with me – no he can't'. Of course, she looked at me as if to say 'why not?' I thought 'I bet she hates me for saying this', and then I thought 'I'm not going to be hated – I'm fed up with people treating me as the ogre, thinking I don't care. Let them know what I think for a change'. So I said 'I'll tell you why'.

I think she wondered what the hell was going on. She took me to the bathroom because there was nowhere else to go, and I just poured everything out.

I couldn't possibly have him to stay with me. To actually have to care for him was out of the question. As I left she said 'let me take his clothes and we'll sort him out. You go on, it would be silly for you to go and see him'. She was really understanding, which I was quite surprised at. When I went in the next day I still didn't know what I was going to say about why I hadn't stayed the day before. He was hardly talking to me and I was hardly talking to him. Another nurse came up and said 'the social worker would like a word with you on the way out – you would like to see her, wouldn't you?' She had seen me go out in tears the day before and realised I was upset, and wanted to know why, so I went into her office. She was the next person I told – she was really understanding and sympathetic, and was the one who persuaded me to join the group.

'I love my sister dearly but she's got everything – a husband, children, a nice home, a good job, no worries. That probably sounds as if I'm jealous but I'm not – it's just that she's never had anything go wrong in her life, so she kept looking at me saying 'you're never satisfied, you'll always want more, you should be happy with what you've got'. It was bugging me that she didn't know. One day I said 'do you want to know why I am so fed up with you saying that? One day I'll tell you'. But I couldn't tell her because I didn't want to destroy what she has had with my father, silly as that may be. I thought 'if she knows, it is going to make a difference', and I still didn't tell her. Eventually, after she went on at me again I told her, and she just didn't know what to do or say. She just started to cry and said 'I did wonder what happened'. I asked her if it had happened to her – she said 'no'.

She knew I was surprised when she told her husband because he is prim – he wouldn't take that sort of thing, he doesn't feel bad about anybody. She told him I had given dad a letter and he just said 'oh' and walked out because that was the easiest way to handle it. He just turned round and walked out – he didn't want to know.

My daughter said 'Mum, I wish you would stop treating me like a child – whatever's going on, I'm fed up with it'. I said 'it is time you knew then'. It was damned hard I can tell you – she looked devastated. She had to know really because my dad wouldn't be coming round and she would want to know where he was. The next day I went to Exeter to tell my married daughter – she was even more devastated but said she understood much more now. It explained a lot – daft things that I had done and it was good that I was able to tell her.

I'd had problems with my brother. He came round just after all this and started telling me off, saying 'I don't know how you can dump Dad like you did. I can understand why you don't want him to stay – I just don't understand why you dumped him'. I said 'you'd better sit down and I'll tell you why – I'm fed up with all of you thinking I'm always in the wrong. It is about time you listened to me'. He said 'I believe you but I don't want to believe you'. Obviously, it took him a while to digest it and a long time to come round to see me again. Even today, I don't think he really believes me. I asked him last year and he said 'I think so, but I don't want to believe it'. It bothered me but I thought 'it happened and that is it'.

As Sue has described, disclosure can bring a variety of responses, from shock and sadness to denial. She had attempted to tell someone outside the family: 'I tried to tell my doctor when I was feeling very depressed in my early 20's – I just pushed it away as he didn't want to know.'

Regardless of the response, telling the truth can be an empowering experience. Disclosure to the family will arouse strong feelings in the survivor – she may fantasise about the outcome but in reality most families respond with denial or minimisation, the mechanisms they used at the time, and tend to carry on as if nothing as happened. As a child, the survivor may have tried to disclose and learned it would not change anything. This was Carol's experience: 'I told a friend and her father called the police. They came but my mother begged me to lie because she couldn't cope on her own. My sister was only little. I told her a few years ago. She then told me he did it to her twice – I cried, I could have stopped that. I told my brother during my healing – he has cut himself of from Mum and Dad.'

Telling those close to you can be frightening for them.

They have to re-evaluate their ideas of who you are and, if he is known to them, the abuser. They also have to find ways of coping with their feelings towards the abuser. This may mean that at the moment you want their love, understanding and support they become too involved in their own process to meet your needs.

Initially Julia told her husband about her father abusing her and he found it difficult to cope with. Then she began to retrieve memories of ritual abuse. She says: 'Finding out about the ritual abuse seems to have forced him to believe in the incest, so he is now more disgusted by that. However, he is more worried about how it affects him, how it has spoiled his memory of my father and how he feels I was foisted on him by my parents as 'damaged goods'. He finds it very hard to see things from my point view, though he does try.'

Recovering memories of abuse had an enormous impact on Julia's life and she wanted her family to be aware of what was happening to her. She, too, discovered that individuals responded differently. 'I told my daughter, (not details) who was extremely supportive, and my youngest son (19), who was at first literally shocked and tearful, then, when he realised I was OK now and he didn't have to make me better, he relaxed and seems to be coping well. I told my older sister who finally agreed to believe me – a very important step forward for me – but she said she would not want to speak of it again, which she hasn't. My brother refused to believe me but thought it was not impossible. My husband blurted some of it out to my cousin and her husband (his brother). It was met with belief and guarded support from my cousin which has since been retracted. Her husband was abusive, disbelieving and cruel – 'stop all this self pitying, what does it matter anyway – you're all right now'. If I had realised he was completely overloaded I would not have told him. My husband hasn't really taken it in so he tried to offload it on to his brother.

The details of the ritual abuse have only been shared with my counsellor. Two friends have been supportive but unable to believe fully – I have only given a broad outline. I have become much more careful who I speak to. Maybe I've finally learned to protect myself from further abuse!'

INNER CHILD

> The nicest thing that my counsellor has said to me so far is that if my child (the child within) could see me now she would be proud of what I am doing!' *Julia*

You may feel, having reached adulthood, that you can leave your childhood behind, but deep inside you is the little girl who lived through the abuse. She holds all the feelings of pain, insecurity, fear, confusion, terror and all the tears resulting from her ordeal.

This 'inner child' is described as 'the part of each of us which is ultimately alive, energetic, creative, and fulfilled; it is our Real Self – who we truly are.'* She is open, feeling, trusting, vulnerable, has the ability to have fun and play, show feelings when they arise and is free to grow and unfold. The inner child is also the part of us which is 'connected to the longings and pain of childhood'.†

When you were abused you learned to disown your inner child by adapting to others. You may have become self critical, withdrawn and without joy, intimacy, creativity and spontaneity. You developed a 'false self', one which was acceptable to your family and which helped you to survive. You couldn't show your real self because you had learned it wasn't acceptable. The false self becomes what the child and ultimately the woman feels she SHOULD be.

* *Healing the Child Within*, Whitfield C L, Deerfield Beech Communications, 1989.
† *The Courage to Heal*, Ellen Bass and Laura Davis.

All the time the false self is used – the Inner Child the real self – remains concealed and prevented from expressing herself. She has been wounded. She had to keep the family secret and so neglect her needs and bypass her true feelings resulting in a build up of unresolved and unfinished business. As an adult the survivor feels empty and numb – never completely whole.

In the 'good enough' family the Inner Child has been allowed to prosper because it has received enough attention, love, touch, acceptance. She has been allowed to show her feelings, trust, have fun, develop her sexuality naturally and has been looked after.

When we have disregarded and ignored our Inner Child for a long time it is hard to know she is really there. She is not always easily accessed because she has had to hide for so long and sometimes has split off completely. Often women pretend that their inner child isn't there and that her feelings do not exist. Or they separate from her, blaming the child they once were for letting the abuse happen or rebuking her for not being strong enough to tell or run away. Carole always discarded her real self because she felt it to be worthless, flawed and irreparable – she didn't believe people would want to know her if they REALLY knew what she was like.

It took Carole a long time to understand she had an inner child and longer for her to acknowledge that this part of herself was lovable and worthy and that Carole needed to befriend her, love her, listen to her feelings and look after her.

Sometimes the true self is seen in glimpses in adulthood. Donna talks about letting go during sex 'I think I only let go once and I was so shocked at myself that I've never done it since. I thought at the time. How dare you? I remember afterwards crying and thinking 'Oh God'. The bloke looked at me and said 'I must have touched a nerve' that is all he said and I thought 'if you only knew'. In situations like this the woman often feels the need to tighten her control even more, hiding away the inner child.

The Inner Child will, until healing has taken place, live in fear of the abuse re-occurring. She remains frightened and finds it difficult to cope with her reality i.e. a woman walking down the road seeing a man who resembles her abuser will experience the feeling of panic and scare even thought she knows it isn't the abuser. It is her child within who feels the panic and scare.

Carole experienced something similar when she bathed, she had to have someone accompany her or leave the door open because her Inner Child feelings were activated. 'The fear in the bath was not of drowning but a fear that something awful was about to happen'. Carole couldn't understand why she felt the way she did until she was able to connect her present day feelings with her experience of being abused in the bathroom.

Carole also says: 'Though I love the countryside I sometimes feel claustrophobic among trees because I was often taken to the woods.'

Accessing her Inner Child was crucial for her healing process. Carole had to be reunited with her Inner child so that she could understand the experience from an adult perspective. She also had to repair the damage and hurts of childhood and give her real self a voice and permission to grieve for the losses sustained in childhood. By doing this she could begin to fulfil her unmet needs.

Carole could become the good, loving and wise parent to her child which she never had. This is known as reparenting.

If you find it difficult to access the little child within you, you might begin by remembering yourself as a child when you needed to be loved and protected. Try to build up a visual image of yourself, what did you look like, your expression, the way you were dressed, how old were you? Keep that image with you, be aware that some of your behaviour, thoughts and feelings are coming from her. Do not be hard on yourself: could you really be hard on this little person? If you are unable to visualise yourself look at little children who are known to you and imagine yourself at that age. If you have real difficulty in bringing any image to mind, try to build up a picture by looking at photographs, or asking those who were close to you and cared to describe you as a child. Keep a photograph with you so that you can remind yourself that she is still around and needs taking care of.

Taking responsibility for giving your inner child the love she needs means being the ideal parent you as a child would have liked. As you begin to become more aware of the needs and feelings you may have pushed away as a child and as you begin to face and understand your past, you will became less dependent on looking for approval externally from your work, possessions, food, drugs, relationships, etc. As you face the negative beliefs about yourself that resulted from the abuse you will understand that you did the best you could; the way you were then was just fine. With that understanding – feeling better about yourself – will come the ability to cherish and care for your inner-child. You will become less demanding of your partner, friends and children as you become more able to recognise and meet your needs. Remember you know your inner-child better than anyone else, you understand her language, and can interpret her behaviour. By reclaiming your inner-child you reclaim control over your life.

Our inner-child never grows up, she is always with us. When she begins to heal it allows us to be more spontaneous, creative, and fun. When you first begin to uncover the feelings your child suppressed you may feel overwhelmed and believe you will not survive the pain. You may feel those feelings will erode any control you have over your life, that you will become dependent on people who may not be able to take proper care of you. It is important to remember that you now have the adult skills you did not have as a child, you have the ability to protect yourself and make things safe, you can set boundaries for your child as we suggested at the beginning of the book. One of those adult skills is the ability to seek help when you feel that the needs of your child are too big for you to cope with.

A way of nurturing your inner-child is to have a dialogue with her. This can be an imaginary conversation between the adult part of yourself and your child, or you may wish to write to her. In this way you can reassure and comfort her. You may like to experience some of the things that you missed out on as a child. You may go to the park and swing as high as you can, work your way through all the ice-cream flavours, buy her a special toy which will provide comfort during the scary and sad times.

During her group therapy Carole on several occasions accessed her inner child feelings when describing a situation she had been in. Other members of the group were able to re-enact the scene from her past so that Carole could call on a 'good parent' to protect little Carole. You can replay the flashbacks or dreams and visualise the situation the way you would have liked it. You can bring in a 'good parent' to rescue your child.

During her healing Carole also wrote to her inner-child. Although the adult part of her was clear and strong in her determination to face the past and recover, her inner child was often scared and wanting to run away, she needed reassurance and understanding. In this moving letter Carole provides this for the child part of herself that was re-experiencing the feelings from the past..

Dear Carole
What is happening to you now is terrifying, evil, wrong and completely unforgivable. I will help you to stop it – trust me.

You need not be afraid any more There are people to help you, care for you and love you. People who will never let you down.

This man has used you and abused you. It has nothing to do with you. You are not, and never have been, to blame for anything.

It's *your* feelings that are important now. You don't have to protect anyone any more.

Don't be afraid to let someone into your life who will help you heal, help the pain go away and help you feel worthwhile and whole again.

It can be done. It will be hard and painful but it will happen. Be strong and remember you are worth it.

NURTURING

As an adult you may have grown accustomed to not getting your needs met. Realise that you still put everyone else's needs before your own. You may struggle to get those around you to compensate for the lack of love you experienced but find yourself making relationships with others who are as needy as yourself. But ultimately it is your responsibility to make sure that your emotional needs are met. As an adult you can not expect that others will do that for you.

The idea of loving and caring for yourself may seem selfish, you may think you must not make your own emotional needs known, although you do not think that it is selfish to tend to your physical needs, making sure you have food to eat or a roof over your head. Often the childhood cycle is perpetuated by being as neglectful and dismissive of your needs as those who cared for you were. You may try to deny the feelings of fear and insecurity and the desperate need for love.

Our society assigns women the role of caretaker. They are expected to be aware of and take care of others' needs. The message to women is not to put her needs first. Child sexual abuse compounds this message – the child learns to take care of others. As an adult the survivor feels not entitled to have her needs met and therefore often feels no resentment. Feelings of guilt, self-blame, and shame may increase her feelings of being unworthy to have her needs met. It may seem very difficult to get the balance right, to take care of others' needs but not at the expense of our own, and to meet our own needs but not at the expense of others'.

Often women who have been abused find it difficult to identify what their needs are. As children they had to deny them in order to survive – although they may be super sensitive to the needs of others. Many describe themselves as being good listeners, an understanding and supportive friend, etc.

As you begin to heal and see yourself not as 'bad' and responsible but as a victim of a powerful adult you will be able to define yourself not through your past, but through what you are making of yourself – your potential. You will begin to reclaim your self-esteem and realise that you have needs and that you can give yourself time to fulfil these, and are able to ask others to meet them too.

You will be able to replace negative beliefs with positive healthier beliefs and attitudes and learn to take care of yourself in ways that up to now you may have been unable to do, or even unaware of. Learning to take care of yourself may not be easy because you were taught that thinking about yourself was selfish. Taking care of yourself does not mean stopping taking care of others, it is finding a balance so you have the time and energy that you deserve to focus on yourself.

To begin with it may be difficult to even allow yourself time to spend on yourself because you do not know what you would like to do with that time. At first set aside a period of time every day, fifteen minutes may be enough to start with, and use that time to focus on yourself, your mind and your body. What does your body need? Relaxation, exercise, time alone?

During the process of healing the women in this book began to take care of themselves, discovering activities which gave them pleasure. For some it was it was having time to themselves to relax and enjoy, Donna says: 'I run a bath and soak and then do my nails and play around with make-up. Sometimes I get dressed up and just go up town for a coffee, sometime I call a friend and meet for lunch.' And for Sue, 'I like my own company at times, I listen to music.'

For others it was leaving the family and enjoying being away from the home. Julia found the countryside healing: 'I go out for the day, especially to the sea or lake – I find water very soothing and the vastness of the sea healing.'

For Tracy it was spending time developing her creativity,

she says: 'I love relaxing with my needle work, I'm forever buying more threads and magazines; that to me is wonderful. To see a finished design on my wall makes me proud of myself which is a new feeling for me and I love it!

MOTHERS

Carole

Before I confronted my father I went to see my mother with Claire – she begged me not to do it. I had to explain why and unfortunately, had to tell her certain things to make it real. I left with her blessing. The arrangement was that we would meet and keep in touch. Eight months later I had received one letter. I don't particularly want to see her but we do correspond on a superficial level – I like to know she's OK.

I feel very strongly that I couldn't discard her, but I don't miss her at all. It's a horrible thing to say about your mother. I honestly think she feels she can not cope with it. I was worried and sad about that at the time, and I wanted to keep in touch with her. Her attitude at the time of the confrontation was as it had always been – 'we must keep the peace, we must not upset him, I must protect myself, I can't understand why Carole has to rock the boat again after all these years'. I wasn't any more important then than I was when I was six, and I've had enough.

I still feel sorry for her. She should have protected me but she wasn't capable. She was as frightened as I was of my father – he was so violent, a beast of a man. I understand that but I can't forgive her for 'sacrificing me'. She must be suffering, too, but she maintains the cover-up, ignoring again what's happened, and is happy to live life on the 'surface'. I had really strong feelings about her in therapy, but now I don't really care if I see her again.

She hasn't deserved the life she's had – she is kind, and never jealous or envious of anyone. She always sees the good in people first and is always pleased for others when life is good for them. I know she is upset that she didn't look after me properly, which is why I can not hate her or completely abandon her.

Once she had dealt with her father's abuse Carole came to realise her mother had neglected her. She says 'When I started therapy I thought it was my father I had to deal with. I was shocked to find how much my mother actually featured in all of this. We spent a lot of time dealing with my mother's attitude and how I could come to terms with her neglect. It was so hard to face the fact she hadn't protected me. A lot of painful work was done on this – it had to be to help me heal. I'm still surprised at the effect of the part she played in my early life and how much it hurt when I realised and admitted to myself she knew'.

It was too painful for Carole as a child to admit to herself that her mother didn't look after her, so she told herself her mother and her grandmother and other members of the family could not have known .

Looking back as an adult, Carole can see how her mother must have known. How could she NOT know. Carole became inflamed by her father's betrayal of her trust and exploitation of her body, but she could not be angry with her mother. Her overwhelming feeling was one of sadness because she knew her mother could have done little. Carole was sad about that – her anger remains with her father. The reality was that her mother could not, and did not, nurture her or protect her.

Carole, in adulthood, also became aware of the pattern of her parents' sexual relationship. She describes how each Sunday afternoon her father would go upstairs to lie down and sometimes he would be bad tempered on rejoining the family; at other times he was in a reasonable mood. She realised that his good moods were dependent on his wife having gone upstairs with him. Like Carole, her mother and the rest of the family were completely dominated by his needs.

'The most difficult part of the group therapy was the discussion about mothers, and how we felt about them.'
Carol

For most survivors there comes a time when they have to face their feelings about their mother or mother figure. The two main questions the survivor and society asks are: how responsible was she and how involved was she?

Society often lays the blame for abuse with the mother for being frigid, working, ill, unbalanced and so on, but we need to remember there are many men with such partners who do NOT abuse children. When a victim has been abused by her father the stereotypical image of her mother is of a hostile, unloving and frigid woman who causes her husband to find sexual gratification elsewhere. In reality, even in the most troubled marriages most offenders still have sex with their partners, and it is important to remember that abuse is not concerned with sexual need. However, research has shown sexual abuse is more likely in families where the mother is absent, dead or suffering from a serious illness. Regardless of the mother's problems the abuse would not occur if the perpetrator had not chosen to do it. The blame with sexual abuse lies only with the abuser. Blaming the mother only victimises a woman who is often a victim already.

Mothers of survivors often present an image which is different from the stereotype, which can make it even more difficult for the survivor to understand her mother's behaviour. Tracy says of her mother: 'My mum was very "perfect". We all had to have standards, keep things clean and keep quiet. She hated any fuss. She wasn't an alcoholic but she did have a problem in that if she mixed with friends socially she would drink far too much and embarrass us all. I think now that she was hiding her problems. My mother should have been there for me and realised what was happening, but she wasn't.'

The survivor's feelings for her mother can be strong and confusing. The natural inclination is to protect the mother and believe she could not have had anything to do with the abuse. This is often the most painful recognition to make, admitting to yourself that your mother was not there for you. There comes a time in most survivors' healing process when they ask 'did she know?' There are several responses to that question – she may have had no knowledge of the abuse, she may have had an awareness but not learned more, she may have known all about it but done nothing, or she may have known and condoned it.

If your mother did know you will have to deal with all the emotions that knowledge brings. Survivors have often had a fantasy that if their mother knew she would have done something to stop the abuse. Giving up this fantasy can be as painful as dealing with your feelings about the abuser. As Tracy says: 'Realising my mum could have helped me, during or after, and knowing she didn't, hurt me deeply. I never saw my mum for who she really was – it was as though I saw her for what I wanted her to be – a perfect mum. When I realised she wasn't it took a lot of talking, writing poems and crying to get through it – that was the worst part of my healing.'

For some survivors, realising their mother refused to act on the knowledge that their daughter was being abused is devastating. Carol describes her experience: 'I never really realised until the session on mothers just how much I blamed my mother for not protecting me. She made me lie to the police to cover for my father. They used to tell me off for lying when it was my mother who made me lie – I really had my whole world turned upside down remembering that incident. I hated my mother but morally I couldn't, as we are taught to 'honour thy mother and father'. Well, I don't and I don't think I ever will. She said 'think of your little sister' – well I tell you now that was the hardest part. A few years ago my younger sister told me he did it to her, too. She is doing her healing now. I felt guilty over that, too. Now the blame goes fairly and squarely where it belongs – at the feet of my father and mother. It has all come out within the family. My sister told my mum what happened to her. My mother broke down and took it all very hard. Our relationship is very much up in the air at the moment. She has apologised to me for all the pain and misery they have put me through over the years. I still love my parents but I have to say at this moment in time I don't like either of them very much.

If the mother was not aware, this leads to further questions – why didn't she know, where was she, why didn't she see the signs? It is common at this time for survivors to have overwhelming feelings of being unimportant and unloved. The reasons for your mother's behaviour will be complex, but do not discount your own feelings.

Mothers of victims are often vulnerable themselves. Some will have been sexually abused themselves as children. It is unlikely that they will have come from 'good enough' families. Not having role models with nurturing and caring attitudes means they may repeat old patterns. Julia is aware that her mother was inadequate in her mothering, but is equally aware that she is following a different pattern. 'I don't think she knew on the conscious level. I don't know how she would have coped if she had. She was unable to cope with her children's pain – she was a child herself, almost certainly abused by an uncle, perhaps also by her mother. I feel she never loved any of us but looked after us well to show she was a "good" mother. I know I am a lot like her, though I do love my children and would die for them, so in that way I am not like her. I know I have more to find out about this relationship.'

If she lacked love, support and nurturing, the mother is likely to choose an emotionally inadequate partner. She can not rescue her child because she does not have the ability to save herself from an inadequate relationship. She may be as emotionally inadequate as her partner, shutting out painful information and putting a wall round the subject, sometimes for the rest of her life.

A mother from a 'not good enough' family is usually oppressed, dependent and subservient – her independent survival seems quite impossible. Rather than provoke her husband's anger or risk his desertion, she will capitulate. If the price she pays is her daughter's safety and well-being, she will not resist. She has no choice but to remain loyal to her husband despite his behaviour. Her collusion with him is a measure of her powerlessness, but no neglect on her part excuses the abuse.

Tracy says: 'I feel for my mum but can't forgive. I don't understand why she's still with him'.

Most victims will have longed for their mothers to come to their rescue, but in reality even if they acknowledge the abuse, they are usually unable to defend their daughter. When their husband is the offender they may initially support their daughter but then shift their allegiance back to the abuser. The individual reasons for the father to become abusive and the mother to become non-protective, or, when the abuse took place outside the family, for them both to become non-protective, are varied. Both parents may have been physically or sexually abused themselves. Their individual life experience may make their reactions understandable and explain why they choose each other as partners. They often recreate the family pattern of their own family of origin.

Survivors often feel abandoned by their mother and exploited by the abuser. It is often easier for them to be angry with their mother, tending to fear or over-idealise the man, rather than be angry with him. It is understandable and right that you feel anger towards the person who failed to protect you, but the abuser deserves your anger, too.

You will also have to grieve for your little child who was abandoned, and whose needs were not recognised or acted upon. As with the abuser, understanding why someone behaved in a certain way does not mean you have to forgive them. That is YOUR choice.

CONFRONTATION

Carole

My father was so powerful that even after prison he was still 'in charge'. I was frightened of him long distance, of his power over me and my life. One day, after I was married, I obeyed him when he told me I used too much make-up. He didn't ask to come to lunch every Saturday – he TOLD me he was coming. It didn't occur to me to argue the point or consider not being there. I broke away from my parents because I gradually realised I had been treated so badly – I hated being in their company. I was scared to say so for a long time but the group work got me there. Eventually, this led to confrontation. My mother tried to stop the confrontation many times. She would ask 'why do you have to bring all this up now when it happened so long ago?' She wanted me to wait until she was dead. She was afraid – the system had to stay closed. She just wanted peace, as usual.

In April 1992, after 35 years, accompanied by my friend, I told my father what his abuse had done to me. I felt I had given back the pain for him to live with now. I was able to tell him I was no longer afraid of him. It was a wonderful feeling knowing it was actually true. Having the strength of Claire's support was crucial. He admitted the abuse and I heard his first words of remorse. I was 52 years old.

Confrontation is a personal decision. For Carole, it was necessary to disclose to several members of her family, and confront her mother before she confronted her father. The reasons can be varied but it is often not done to gain an apology – it is highly unlikely that the abuser will accept the blame. Carole demonstrated so bravely how she would not be silenced. She would not carry the secrets of her family any longer, and she handed him back the guilt and the shame. She was able to face her fear head-on and take back the power her father had robbed her of for so many years. She was able, with her therapists and with the support of her fellow group members to prepare for the confrontation. Role playing was used to anticipate her father's possible reactions – anger, denial and so on. We also stipulated that she was accompanied by another member of the group for support and safety.

Unlike some parts of the recovery process, confrontation like Carole's is not essential to healing. You can heal without it. You need to give a great deal of thought to why you want to confront the abuser, examining your motivation, hopes and needs. It is unlikely that you will feel strong enough to take this step early in your recovery. It needs to be done from a position of power, which will come as you heal. You may decide confrontation will never be in your best interests and that is OK. By confronting the abuser you reject the role of the secret-bearer, and you make the abuser and your family aware that you will no longer take responsibility for their behaviour.

Survivors rarely receive the response they are looking for and you should be prepared for that. It is important to remember that YOU, not your family, have changed.

When the abuser is the father or father figure, the survivor wants her parents to take responsibility for their behaviour – her father for the abuse and her mother for neglecting to provide protection. Ideally, they will then show regret, apologise and make amends for the wrong done to her.

The more disclosure which has been made prior to the confrontation the more validated the survivor will feel in confronting the abuser and the more likely her family is to provide support.

Survivors need to decide which is the best way to carry out the confrontation, face to face, by letter or on the telephone. If you think confronting the abuser face to face could put you at risk of violence, a letter or phone call gives you protection. The disadvantage is that there may be no response to a letter and a phone call can be cut off by the abuser. If the abuser is now dead, or has always been unknown to you, letter writing can be used. Writing down how you feel about the abuser and what he did to you can be therapeutic. One anonymous woman's confrontation of the abuser, her uncle, was made by letter: 'After 12 months of healing I wrote him a letter and received a reply admitting guilt. He promised he would not return to this area and respected my wish not to make the abuse public knowledge.'

The survivor will probably fear, and perhaps wish, that something terrible will happen as a result of confronting the abuser – he may have a heart attack, his wife may divorce him, the family may become so enraged they do him physical harm. In reality, their defence mechanisms make these conclusions unlikely. Sue feared her father might have a heart attack when she confronted him by letter: 'When my father was due to come out of hospital I thought 'I am going to disown him. I wrote him a letter and decided to ask the nurses to keep an eye on him. They could sort it out – I really didn't care if he had a heart attack. I took the letter in on a Saturday morning, I walked in with this little letter and asked the nurse 'Can you give him this and please could you watch him while he is opening it. Again, I was looking after him. I explained what was in it and walked out of there.'

Later on Sue sent her father a letter telling him exactly how she felt: 'What happened years ago has affected me badly but I'm going to come to terms with it. I've got to, or what else have I got? I don't speak to you now – I can't and I don't want to. I thought I hated you a few months ago but now I don't know. I hated what you did and will never know why it was me. It was wicked and you should never have done this to me. You robbed me of my youth and part of my life, with your greed and selfishness. No parent should have done what you did – you weren't a man. A father should be looked up to, but how can I respect a person who used me and has destroyed part of me.'

Though confrontation is best carried out with careful planning and preparation, the chance to confront the abuser sometimes comes unexpectedly, in a surprise meeting or when you suddenly find yourself alone with him. In a letter to her father, Sue describes bumping into him in the town where they both lived: 'I saw you the other day but you looked away and disappeared. You know what you have done but still you remain silent. Then there you were, face to face with me. You looked weird. Somehow I didn't know what to say so I just said 'Hi ya', like one does as if nothing has happened. Should I stop? I just kept talking – you were gobsmacked I'd say. I asked 'how are you.' You said 'fine' – you didn't look it. You said: 'I've been so worried about you'. 'Oh yeah,' I said – I didn't mean it nastily. You asked if I wanted coffee. I said 'no, I haven't time' – I really didn't. In the end I said goodbye, and as I turned to go I said 'I only wish you could have said sorry'. That was it. You were so humble 'I'm sorry, I'm sorry' I heard you say. 'I'm so sorry. I wouldn't have upset you for the world'. But you'd done that. I turned to go. I can't remember much after that until I saw you rushing towards me. You were saying sorry, grabbing my hands. 'I am truly, truly sorry' you said. I was embar-rassed now and wanted to go. You were crying. I didn't know what to say or do, so I just said 'OK, that's OK, I'll see you soon', then you walked away. I turned to go. I was in a daze. I got out of the shop and could breathe again – the air was clear. It was cold and I walked away. I felt better after seeing you – now that bit is over. I will see you sometime but I don't know when. I'm still hurting – I still don't understand why it was me. I don't suppose I'll ever know the reason WHY – do you know? You phoned me a couple of times lately and I can now speak to you without feeling threatened – that's good. I now see you as an old man who is broken. It is so, so sad, when we could have had so much. Mum is now gone. I often think about her and wonder if she ever knew – I hope not.'

You need to be realistic about the kind of response you might receive from the abuser. It is unlikely that he will put your needs first – he was not able to do so in the past. He may respond with denial or an ambiguous response – 'I can't remember but I'm sure I wouldn't do anything like that.' He may acknowledge the abuse but not accept responsibility or express remorse. He may use minimisation – 'it happened but it was a long time ago and it didn't hurt anyone'. He may try to blame you, suggesting you liked it or wanted it to happen. Another ploy is to try to put you on his side by admitting it happened and he has a problem, but at the same time giving you good reasons why it needs to be kept secret, appealing to your loyalty to prevent other people being hurt. The abuser may also use more frightening ways to acknowledge the abuse, admitting the abuse but challenging you in a threatening way by asking 'and what are you going to do about it?'. Occasionally, after admitting responsibility, he may even try to perpetuate the abuse by turning remorseful affection into fondling or attempted rape. This was Tracy's experience: 'After I was married with my own family I confronted him on the phone. I called him all the names under the sun, told him what I thought of him and then asked him why he did it. He said: 'I fancy you more than your mother – aren't I a naughty Daddy'. Those words will haunt me for the rest of my life – I hate him.'

If you confront the abuser and he denies that the abuse took place it is likely that his family will support him. If they were unaware of the abuse they may be shocked and unable to cope with the information. They may side with him and turn you into a scapegoat, convincing themselves that you are lying or that, if it did happen, it was your fault.

When confronted, the abuser may acknowledge and apologise for the abuse. You are under no obligation to respond to an apology – his expectation may be that you will forgive him, but you do not have to fulfil that. You need time to consider what his apology means to you and whether you are willing to accept it. What does his apology mean? Can it be trusted? Remember, you have been told lies before. You are the one who has put so much energy into changing, so it is unlikely that he has done the same. You may decide never to see the abuser again once you have confronted him, or, if you feel you have received a satisfactory response, to start building a new relationship with him. Bear in mind what you have learned about the abuser; sexual abuse is an act of a dysfunctional person.

Another possibility is that the abuser may admit responsibility at the time, and even show remorse and make promises about the future, but then a few days later retract it all and try again to blame you for his behaviour, suggesting you 'made him' say those things which were not true. This may make you feel a little crazy. It is important to remember that sexual abuse is perpetrated by men who are not well developed, functioning individuals, so you can expect their behaviour to be strange.

After the confrontation, be gentle with yourself: take time to allow yourself to react to the process. You may find you are initially exhilarated, and then frightened or disappointed. You will probably need extra support and a chance to talk things over at this point. It will probably be some time before you understand the full impact of the confrontation. Meanwhile do things you really like and which remind you that there is a life beyond the abuse.

HOW TO CONFRONT YOUR ABUSER

Only attempt to confront the abuser when YOU feel ready. Do not be persuaded by anyone that it is the 'next step'. The more secure you feel about yourself the more able you will be to cope with the possible difficulties which arise. It is OK to change your mind or put it off until another time when you feel stronger and more powerful.

Try to make sure the abuser will be on his own when you confront him. If you have a therapist, you can invite him to a session with you both. If you are approaching the abuser in his home, consider taking a friend with you. Make a plan to cope with the abuser's family if you can not confront him alone. Decide how you will approach them so that they will respect your need to have time alone with him.

Decide in advance what you want to say. If you have a therapist or belong to a survivors' group you can role play the confrontation – this will help you prepare your responses and anticipate any difficulties. Make your statements specific and straightforward: 'I am angry with you for what you did'. He may respond with denial. Be prepared with this statement: 'I know you abused me – I can remember what happened.' Then give specific details – age, time, place and what was done. He may try to say you were responsible, so tell him what you have learned about the abilities of a child and the responsibilities of an adult.

The abuser will try to take the power back. This is expected, as having power and control has been his primary need. You need to protect yourself, so take someone you trust with you – if they do not come into the room with you make sure they are nearby. Be clear about how long it will take you to say what you want to say. Once that time has elapsed have the person come in to check things out. The abuser will probably use blackmail to try to maintain the secrecy and force you back into a state of powerlessness. You may doubt your own reality. He may hook the little child in you, who may begin to believe all those things she was told before. You could take a tape recorder with you so you can listen to what was said afterwards and review it from a calm, adult perspective. Carole had Claire with her throughout the confrontation with her father. She was able to remind her of what was said and be a 'good enough parent' to her in the hours which followed.

Consider any questions you want to ask the abuser, and be aware that he make take the opportunity to try to justify his behaviour. He may also become angry or upset, and ask for forgiveness. Either way, refuse to listen and leave.

Consider how you might deal with your emotions. If possible, try to release feelings of anger or sadness with your therapist or group members before you confront the abuser. If you are working through your healing by yourself, tell your partner or the person who supports you what you intend to do and explore your feelings with them. You may also find release in writing down everything you would like to say to the abuser if you could have him gagged and standing in front of you. If you fear you may become overwhelmed by your feelings during the confrontation, take a letter with you saying exactly what you want to say face to face. If you are unable to stay you can hand it to him before you go.

Be clear about how you are going to reply to his response, and be prepared for all possibilities. Decide how YOU want to leave things, regardless of how he responds. Plan for some recovery time and be aware that you may feel shaken after breaking such an entrenched childhood pattern. You will be breaking major rules from your childhood which were made as survival decisions, so you may feel the 'real' fear of your child. For Carole, this was a return to herself as a six-year-old the day after the confrontation. She felt all the fear and vulnerability returning, and fully expected her father to take revenge and kill her, as he had threatened to do when she was a child. With support, she was able to return to her adult state and KNOW he was not able to do this now – he was not the powerful man of her childhood.

Carole now has the skills to stop looking at her father through the eyes of a child, but through the eyes of the powerful adult she now is. She does not have to please him now and keep him in a good mood. She now has choice: she is in control of her life and the quality of her relationships with others.

REFLECTION

This is not an easy book to read and it has not been an easy book to write. Although we are not survivors our experience of writing this book has in may ways paralleled the experience of healing – it was a painful journey and a difficult one. Many times we faced what seemed to be insurmountable problems and on occasion feared we would not get through it.

The book took us over two years to complete when our contract was for one year, but the bonus in this is that we have continued to watch Carole come to terms with her past and start to experience some of the love, joy and respect she so completely missed out on as a child.

One of the major changes during this time was the death of Carole's father. Without preparation Carole had to face and challenge her family's expectations of her. Carole had to deal with an array of feelings and as before she turned to poetry to express herslef and to mark another milestone of her healing.

Yesterday a tyrant died, dead at last for real.
Now I'm left in total shock, afraid of how I feel.

This has released us all from hell, especially my
mother.
But he is the one who's now at peace, no feelings
left to smother.

Feeling used and worthless was, by far, the worst.
I wish it had been different and just once I had
come first.

But she was weak and fearful, though I hope that
she did try
But before she could acknowledge me, first he had
to die.

He should have died in agony, in body and in
　　mind
For all the pain inflicted on those he left behind.

But life's not like that, fate sometimes takes a hand.
It's not always fair and just, and we must try to
　　understand.

We're taught from childhood to be sad, when
　　someone has to die
But it wasn't sadness yesterday – just relief that
　　made me cry.

Then I cried for feeling wicked and I cried for
　　feeling glad
And I cried for all the loving care I never, ever had.

Well I can never change that so, no point dwelling
　　on the past.
I give myself permission to be glad he's gone at
　　last.

Though to me he has been dead some time, almost
　　two years I'd say,
When all my fear just left me on that special April
　　day.

My memories are a problem, they never go away
But I live in hope that NOW, they'll be fading day
　　by day.

I've so much now to live for, life get's better all the
　　time
And in my heart I know, to rejoice is not a crime.

BIBLIOGRAPHY

Angelou, M. (1984) *I know why the caged bird sings*, Virago, London.

Bass, E. and Davies, L. (1988) *The Courage to heal*, Harper and Row, New York.

Bass, E. and Thornton, L. (Eds.) (1983) *I never told anyone: Writings by women survivors of child sexual abuse*, Harper and Row, New York.

Berne, E. (1975) *Transactionalanalysis in Psychotherapy*, Souvenir Press.

Black, C. (1982) *It will never happen to me*, M.A.C., Denver.

Blume, E.S. (1990) *Secret survivors: uncovering incest and its after effects in women*, John Wiley and Sons, New York.

Bradshaw, J. (1990) *Homecoming: reclaiming and championing your inner child*, Piatkus, Great Britain.

Clarkson, P. (1991) *Transactional Analysis: An integrated approach*, Routledge.

Davis, L. (1990) *The Courage to Heal Workbook*, Harper Row, New York.

Davis, L. (1991) *Allies in Healing: when the person you love was sexually abused as a child*, Harper Collins, New York.

Donaldson, M. (1978) *Children's Minds*, Fontana Press, Great Britain.

Draucker, C.B. (1992) *Counselling Survivors of childhood sexual abuse*, Sage, London.

Engel, B. (1989) *The Right to Innocence: Healing the trauma of child sexual abuse*, J.P. Tarcher, Los Angeles.

Erskine, R.G. and Moursand, J.P. (1988) *Integrative Psychotherapy in Action*, Sage, London.

Ernst, S. and Goodison, L. (1981) *In our hands: A woman's book of self help therapy*, Women's Press, London.

Forward, S. and Buck, C. (1979) *Betrayal of innocence. Incest and its devastation*, Penguin Books, New York.

Furness, T. (1991) *The Multi-Professional Handbook of Child Sexual Abuse: Integrated Management therapy and legal intervention*, Routledge, Canada.

Grubman-Black, S.D. (1990) *Broken Boys Mending Men: Recovery of childhood sexual abuse*, HSI and TAB McGraw-Hill, USA.

Hall, L. and Lloyd, S. (1989) *Surviving Child sexual abuse: The handbook for helping women challenge their past*, The Falmer Press, Basingstoke.

Harris, T.A. (1973) *I'm OK Your're OK*, Pan.

Herman, J.L. (1981) *Father-daughter incest*, Harvard University Press, Cambridge.

Hewson, J. and Turner, C. (1992) *Transactional Analysis in Management*, The Staff College, Bristol.

James, M. and Jongeward, D. (1978) *Born to win: Transactional analysis with Gestalt experiments*, Signet Books, New York.

Jehu, D. (1988) *Beyond Sexual Abuse: Therapy with women who were childhood victims*, J. Wiley and Sons, london.

Kitzinger, S. (1985) *Woman's experience of sex*, Pelican, Harmondsworth.

Klein, M. (1980) *Lives people live: Textbook of Transactional Analysis*, Wiley, London.

Levin, P. (1988) *Cycles of power*, Health Communications Inc. Deerfield Beach, Fl.,

Lew, M. (1988) *Victims no longer: Men recovering from incest and other sexual child abuse*, Harper and Row, New York.

Maltz, W. and Holman, B. (1987) *Incest and Sexuality: A guide to understanding and healing*, Lexington Books, Lexington.

Miller, A. (1987) *The drama of being a child, the search for the true self*, Virago, London.

Miller, A. (1983) *For your own good: Hidden cruelty in childrearing and the roots of violence*, Farrar, Strauss and Giroux, New York.

Miller, A. (1984) *Thou shalt not be aware. Society's betrayal of the child*, Pluto, London.

Morris, M. (1984) *If I should die before I wake*, Black Swan, London.

Phillips, A. and Rakusen, J. (1978) *Our bodies, ourselves*, Penguin, Harmondsworth.

Parkes, P. (1990) *Rescuing the 'inner child': therapy for adults sexually abused as children*, Souvenir Press, Great Britain.

Sanford, L. (1991) *Strong at the Broken places: overcoming the Trauma of childhood sexual abuse*, Virago, London.

Sgroi, S. (1982) *Handbook of Clinical intervention in child sexual abuse*, Lexington Books, Cambridge.

Spring, J. (1987) *Cry Hard and swim*, Virago, London.

Steiner, C. (1974) *Scripts People Live*, Grove Press,

Stewart, I. and Joines, V. (1989) *T.A. Today: A new introduction to Transactional Analysis*, Lifespace,

Tebo, B. and Tebo, T. (1993) *Free to be me*, Bantam, Sydney.

Utain, M. and Oliver, B. (1989) *Scream Louder: Through hell and healing with an incest survivor and her therapist*, Health Communications Inc., Florida.

Walker, A. (1982) *The Color Purple*, Pocket Books, New York.
Westerlund, E. (1992) *Women's sexuality after childhood incest*,
   New York.

INDEX